Love —
It's The Greatest!

Love —
It's The Greatest!

Rev. Dr. John H. Krahn

CSS Publishing Company, Inc.
Lima, Ohio

LOVE — IT'S THE GREATEST!

First Edition
Copyright © 2019
by CSS Publishing Co., Inc.

Library of Congress Cataloging-in-Publication Data
Names: Krahn, John H., 1943- author. Title: Love, it's the greatest / John Krahn. Description: FIRST EDITION. | Lima: CSS Publishing Company, Inc., 2019. Identifiers: LCCN 2018039966 | ISBN 9780788029301 (pbk. : alk. paper) Subjects: LCSH: Love--Biblical teaching. | Bible. Corinthians, 1st, XIII--Criticism, interpretation, etc. Classification: LCC BS2675.6.L6 K73 2019 | DDC 241/.4--dc23

e-book:
ISBN-13: 978-0-7880-2931-8
ISBN-10: 0-7880-2931-2

ISBN-13: 978-0-7880-2930-1
ISBN-10: 0-7880-2930-4

Love —
It's The Greatest!

Rev. Dr. John H. Krahn

CSS Publishing Company, Inc.
Lima, Ohio

LOVE — IT'S THE GREATEST!

First Edition
Copyright © 2019
by CSS Publishing Co., Inc.

Library of Congress Cataloging-in-Publication Data
Names: Krahn, John H., 1943- author. Title: Love, it's the greatest / John Krahn.
Description: FIRST EDITION. | Lima: CSS Publishing Company, Inc., 2019.
Identifiers: LCCN 2018039966 | ISBN 9780788029301 (pbk. : alk. paper) Sub-
jects: LCSH: Love--Biblical teaching. | Bible. Corinthians, 1st, XIII--Criticism,
interpretation, etc. Classification: LCC BS2675.6.L6 K73 2019 | DDC 241/.4--
dc23

---

e-book:
ISBN-13: 978-0-7880-2931-8
ISBN-10: 0-7880-2931-2

ISBN-13: 978-0-7880-2930-1
ISBN-10: 0-7880-2930-4   PRINTED IN USA

Other Titles by John H. Krahn

Living A Happier Life At Every Age!

Special Stories Along Life's Journey

Brief Prayers for Busy Lives

From Surviving to Thriving —
A Practical Guide to Revitalize Your Church

Seasonings for Sermons III

Washed Any Feet Lately?

Reaching the Inactive Member

Ministry Ideabank

Ministry Ideabank II

Ministry Ideabank III

Dedication

This book is dedicated to my Lord Jesus Christ who has loved me unconditionally.

It is also dedicated to those people throughout my long life who have loved me. These include my wife, my children and grandchildren, my sons-in-law, my parents and sister, my brother-in-law, grandparents, aunts and uncles, cousins, nephews and nieces, mentors and friends. Each in their own way has blessed my life with their love. For each and every one of them, I am eternally grateful.

Table of Contents

Introduction

What has happened to love? Is love dead? Or is it, at best, a completely outdated concept? One might be led to think this by much of the vitriol reported in the news and demonstrated especially in recent political contests. What about altruism and forgiveness, which are important aspects of love? These also seem at times to be in short supply.

To write a book on *love* might seem so very untimely in our current culture. Yet, this might just be the time it is needed most. You might be thinking that I am preaching to the choir since you are the one who bought this book. Do not others, who would not even consider purchasing a book like this, need it more? No question about it, but please consider that you might need it as well.

Because love is such a rich concept with many layers, each of us would do well to explore its beauty and usefulness in more depth. Such exploration has a perfect guide in Saint Paul of Tarsus as he outlines what love entails in chapter thirteen of his love letter to the Christians living in Corinth. All of us who are willing to explore love will find ourselves both challenged and encouraged to love more deeply. As we do this, our lives will be enhanced. Loving more completely, others in our lives will also be blessed. Even our world and society will benefit as well.

This book can be beneficial in several ways. It will work very well as a text for a Bible study group. After each chapter are questions for thoughtful reflection and group discussion based on the content. It can also be read individually as a devotional book. Whether using it for a Bible study group or simply as a devotional book, when you read something that is especially meaningful to you, might I suggest that you put a check mark next to it in the book's margin? If there is something that you may not understand or agree with, put a question mark beside this and discuss it with others. Most importantly, put an exclamation point next to something you feel God is encouraging you to do. Write a name in the margin when the text brings a particular person to mind. Again, take time to consider the ten items at the end of each chapter under the title of "Reflection." By accepting this discipline, the book will become an even greater blessing for your life. Be blessed with your love "tune up," and grow deeper in Christian love.

In conclusion, I wish to thank my wife Doris, along with Joann Breitbach, Evelyn Andersen Meyers, and Dr. Astrid Sipos for doing a careful job of proofreading this book and making thoughtful suggestions that have improved it. While doing this, each of these women demonstrated a love that was both generous and kind.

Saint Paul's Love Poem

If I speak in the tongues of mortals and of angels, but do not have love, I am a noisy gong or a clanging cymbal. And if I have prophetic powers, and understand all mysteries and all knowledge, and if I have all faith, so as to remove mountains, but do not have love, I am nothing. If I give away all my possessions, and if I hand over my body to be burned, but do not have love, I gain nothing.

Love is patient; love is kind; love is not envious or boastful or arrogant or rude. It does not insist on its own way; it is not irritable or resentful; it does not rejoice in wrongdoing, but rejoices in the truth. It bears all things, believes all things, hopes all things, endures all things.

Love never ends. But as for prophecies, they will come to an end; as for tongues, they will cease; as for knowledge, it will come to an end. For we know only in part, and we prophesy only in part; but when the complete comes, the partial will come to an end. When I was a child, I spoke like a child, I thought like a child; I reasoned like a child; when I became an adult, I put to an end childish ways. For now we see in a mirror, dimly, but then we will see face to face. Now I know only in part; then I will know fully, even as I have been fully known. And now faith, hope, and love abide, these three; and the greatest of these is love.

1 Corinthians 13 (NRSV)

ONE

Love — The More Excellent Way

Clergy kids are little different than any other kids. Having two children myself, one of the things I soon discovered is that it is often hard to please them. This is especially true when it comes to things like ice cream. Give kids one scoop of ice cream, and they will want two. Give them a double dip, and they will still complain and ask for more. It is just the way of kids.

Once I was scooping ice cream into a bowl for my three-year-old under her watchful eye. I knew whenever I would stop and say, "Here is your ice cream," that she would complain that it was not enough. This time while I was still putting the ice cream in her bowl, I inquired, "How much would you like?" Her eyes lit up as she thought for a moment. She had not been blessed with such an opportunity during the entire three years of her life. She responded, "Give me too much."

As we grow older, few of us lose the desire and allure of having too much out of life. "How much is enough?" Most of us would answer, "A little bit more." Vigorous pursuit of a more successful life and a more excellent way of living has become one of the benchmarks of our day. What are the qualities that make a salesperson excel? What must one do to scamper up the corporate ladder of success? What is the way to achieve the excellence that gets you ahead in life that leads to happiness, well-being, and all of the good stuff we secretly dream about? How can I have more of it and have it quicker? We have an innate quest for more. Why not make our quest one for a greater ability to love as God has loved us? This is a quest worth pursuing.

13

As my two daughters grew to be teenagers, I found myself spending more and more time in shopping malls. In order for all of us to keep our family relationship intact, I had an agreement with my wife and daughters that we would meet one another later at a designated time and place. Having no other children, I was on my own to do what I enjoyed. The bookstore was a favorite place for me to spend my time. All bookstores were laid our pretty much the same. There was always a large section of "how to" books like, How to Buy Real Estate with no Money Down, How to Pay Little or No Taxes, How to Achieve Financial Success.

There was another whole section of "how to make yourself look better" books. The best sellers of all were the diet books. There were the "shape up" books and "how to dress for success" books. Each book jacket beckoned me to purchase it. "Shape up," "dress up," "move up," were all there in abundance.

But there is one "how to" book that has been on the market for well over 1,000 years, and it has always been a best seller. It may well be the original "how to a better, more abundant life," book. It is as timely today as when it was first written. It covers every major aspect of our life and gives positive principles that lead to success and excellence in living. Tried and tested over the centuries, it is the "how to" book that consistently delivers to those who are touched by its message and are changed by its teachings. Yes, we have the how to of "how to" books: the Holy Bible. Within its cover is a treasure trove filled with gems for daily living.

One of the richest deposits of gems is found in the thirteenth chapter of Saint Paul's first letter to the Corinthians. Here we discover an almost poetic treatment of love. In just a few short lines inspired by God, we are instructed in the "how to" of loving. Love is still one of the most popular concepts known to humankind. Love is used in so many ways that its use runs the gamut from romance novels to perfume

14

and even to baby diapers. Love is often called upon to describe so much, and it is stretched so far that the core of its meaning is lost as it is shaped and reshaped by our society. In 1 Corinthians 13, Saint Paul takes us back to the core meaning of love. Remarkably, it takes him only about 300 words to deliver his beautiful treatise on love. His words are almost a poetic interpretation of Jesus' Sermon on the Mount. The love of Saint Paul is like a brilliant diamond of many facets. It instructs us on what a life of love really entails.

God Is Love

The author of love is almighty God. Without God, there is no love. "God is love," (1 John 4:16) the Bible tells us simply. Love is the purest essence of God. If you had to describe God in just one word, *love* would be the best one to choose. God's love for us is not diluted sentimentality or mere fondness because God created us. It is not a soap opera kind of love or merely a passing fantasy. Rather God's love for us is a steadfast love, unshakable and enduring forever. It has permanence and does not take off when the road gets rough. It is loyal. You can count on it being there when you need it.

King Solomon, who had 700 wives and 300 concubines was approached one day by wife 394 who asked, "Honey, do you love me?" to which he replied, "Dearest, you are one in a thousand!" This quip is not true, of course, but one could wonder whether or not Solomon was able to love and please 1,000 women. Yet there is no question that God is capable of loving each and every one of us individually and specially.

Jesus said that not even one hair falls from our head without God taking notice. He said that God even knows the number of hairs on our head. When you comb your hair in the morning, do you count the number of hairs that come out in your comb? Having obtained that number, do you then subtract that from the total number of hairs on your head that

15

you counted the night before? Not even the most narcissistic of us knows the total number of hairs on our head at any given moment. The Bible tells us that the depth of God's caring love even extends that far.

God Loves Unconditionally

God's love, perhaps more than anything else, is a redeeming love. Even when we turn our backs on God again and again, God's love does not quit on us. For you see, God's love is irrational. It is an unconditional love. Our love, on the other hand, is very often conditional. We love if we are loved in return. We forgive hoping to also be forgiven. We give in order to receive. Much of the time our love can be described as an if/then love: "If you do not talk negatively about my family, I will not talk negatively about your family." "If you let me buy this, then I will let you buy that." "If you are nice to me, then I will be nice to you." Love that is regulated by the other person's response is not Christian love at all. As recipients of unconditional love, we cannot, in turn, love conditionally. Can you imagine if God loved us conditionally? "If you always do my will, then I'll listen to your prayers." "If you give generously to the poor, I'll provide for all of your needs." "If you do not sin, I have a place for you in heaven." If God's love was patterned after ours, we would all be headed for hell at our death.

Thankfully God loves with an "even though" kind of love: "Even though you don't always do my will, I will still love and forgive you if you confess and believe in me." While we were sinners, Jesus Christ died for us. He came to love and save us not because we deserved it but because we needed it. And providing for our needs emanates from God's love. God's plan of love and salvation was worked out through the long history of the wayward nation of Israel all the way to the cross. The cross best proclaims the indisputable fact that we worship a loving God.

16

Through the cross, we have possibility beyond the present. We have an eternal future. It provides hope for the hopeless, love for the loveless, encouragement for the depressed, and pronounces life beyond death for those grieving the loss of loved ones. The cross and vacant tomb are central to our faith. Believing in them, we can confidently sing out, "Jesus loves me, this I know."

When I look at the cross, I cannot but remember a movie I saw many years ago. Few movies in my long life have had the impact of *Ben Hur*. Many scenes made an indelible impression — the great sea battle; the exciting chariot race; the repugnant leprosy colony. Yet, none hit me harder than the crucifixion of our Lord. The sound of hammer - on - nail rings through the air; the cross slowly rises until it suddenly thumps hard into the hole prepared to cradle it. Slowly, Jesus' blood begins to flow... one drop, then another... as a puddle begins to form beneath the cross. It begins to rain. Water mixes with more blood until together they begin to trickle down the hillside. The trickle becomes a stream, washing over God's — creation symbolically cleansing it. I was reminded how the blood of Jesus cleanses me from all sin.

The blood of Christ pouring down the cross restored our relationship with God. We cannot fully understand the mystery of God's plan to recapture a creation gone astray. We only know that all who come to the cross in simple, trusting faith are cleansed by Christ's blood and find peace with God.

Unchained From Sin

By his death, Jesus has unchained us from the clutches of our sin. *Unchained* — there is no better word for it. Jesus set us free from the wages of our sins that only pay dividends in hell. Now we are heaven bound and are on a positive pathway to an eternal life with God. Our eyes need no longer be downcast; our head has no reason to be between our knees. We are no longer oppressed by our weighty sins, for we are loved by none other than almighty God. God loves us not just a little but powerfully. God's love encounters our sin, and it is no more.

But this love story does not end at Calvary. We must proceed to a borrowed tomb that once held Jesus body but was discovered empty just three days later. Emptiness was never more profound or beautiful. Only Easter and Christ's resurrection from the dead had the ability to change that awful Friday before it and make it good for all of us.

Every year, over a million people embark on a spiritual pilgrimage to the holy land to literally walk in the footsteps of our Lord. One of the places that pilgrims particularly enjoy visiting is the garden tomb. This is a site that many believe was the actual tomb of Joseph of Arimathea, where Jesus was buried between Good Friday and Easter Sunday.

On one occasion when I visited the garden tomb, it was at the end of the day. The caretakers were starting to close up as we were completing our communion service. Since the original stone which was rolled in front of the tomb's opening was no longer there, a wooden door has now been fastened discreetly to protect the tomb from possible vandals. The door is not visible when the tomb is open for pilgrims. It was five in the afternoon; as we completed our service, the caretaker closed the wooden door. When he did this, I noticed a portion of scripture that had been written on the face of the door. The scripture chosen was only four words long but was most profound in its simplicity. Quoted were the words of the angel, "He is not here."

I thought, "How do you like that? We traveled thousands of miles and the Lord is not here." In fact, every believer likes it very much. We praise God that the garden tomb is profoundly and magnificently and gloriously empty. For the Lord is risen; he is risen indeed! No longer confined to his earthly body, we know that Jesus is now present with us everywhere. Consider this, all the forces of evil tried to win a victory at Calvary with hammer, nails, and cross. All the spiritual power the religious authorities could muster, and all the earthly power the Roman authorities could amass, were not enough to prevent the Lord from rising from the dead that first Easter morning. Resurrection power was greater than the power of Satan and of evil men.

Resurrection Power Is Ours

Now Saint Paul tells us the same power that propelled Christ from death to life is available to you and me. It gives us the possibility of a new start in those areas of our lives deadened by sin, as well as a new start in renewing relationships hampered by past misunderstandings. The transforming, renewing, recreating power of the resurrected Lord — unleashed that first Easter — is now available for our daily living. It is as available to us as a whispered prayer.

Even more than this, because of God's love in Christ, our powerful resurrected life continues with us into eternity. For those who believe, death is not a period but a comma. It is a pause between our abundant earthly lives in Christ as we make our way to the heavenly life lived in the presence of God. Some critics have said that the church is so heavenly minded that it is of no earthly good. That could be a danger, I guess, but an even greater danger we all face is one of becoming so earthly minded that we chance missing heaven altogether.

As beautiful as Easter is, and as glorious as that first Easter must have been, there is an even more glorious day yet to dawn. It will be that spectacular day when the Risen Lord, the Prince of life, will return in all glory and splendor. He comes to invite those of us who have been faithful to him during our earthly lives to join him in eternity.

On my pilgrimage to Jerusalem, I did not encounter one tomb inscribed: "Here lies Jesus of Nazareth." None exists. Where, then, is the risen Lord? He is everywhere we are.

And where does he wish to reside? He wants to live in our hearts and minds. Jesus' life, death, and resurrection were a visual and profound demonstration of God's love for us. In Jesus of Nazareth, love took on a human face and spoke with a human voice. He joined God the Father and says to each of us, "I love you." Jesus became not only the paradigm of love but — more importantly — the power of love. All believers now have the possibility of loving others with the quality of love which they have first received from the Lord.

Loving Others As We Have Been Loved

When we fall deeply in love with the Lord, we are often amazed at how different we become. There is a new intensity of love for our spouse and children. We discover that the most important thing a father can do for his children is to love their mother. The same holds true for a mother. Even the no-good neighbor is seen in a different light. What we often do not intellectualize is that, through a greater faith and love for the Lord, we will receive a greater indwelling of God who is the source of perfect love. Love lives where God lives. Loving is a joyous and liberating experience. The benefactors of our love are also liberated to love us back. For, you see, love breeds more love in return. Love boomerangs back to us as we freely give it to others.

I like to spell "love" another way. Rather than *LOVE,* I sometimes prefer to spell it *GIVE.* To love is to give ourselves to another person as Christ gave himself for us... unselfishly... without looking to receive something in return. God loves us not because we are worthy of his love, but because we need it. We, in turn, love others out of their need not out of their worthiness. Next, I like to put *FOR* in front of the *GIVE* to further enhance its meaning. To love as Christ did, we must readily and willingly forgive one another.

Sin is the enemy of love. It not only blocks the channels of love between God and us but also between us and others. Who has hurt you? Until you forgive that person, you will not be able to savor the beauty that is locked up in him or her. Forgiveness is the key which unlocks the door of our hearts and allows the gift of love to be given and received again.

The great theologian, Karl Barth, was once asked, "What was the greatest theological truth he has ever read or written about during his long and distinguished career." Without a moment's hesitation, he replied, "Jesus loves me — this I know." In Christ, love has reached down from God to each of us. Receiving God's love in Christ in its fullest, we can enjoy our earthly lives with others more completely. Then, in time, we will be raised from the dead to enjoy life with God forever. In this context, Saint Paul described the more excellent way of love for both the Christians in Corinth as well as for us who are wise enough to embrace his teachings. What the Holy Spirit gives us through the pen of Saint Paul is pure wisdom and treasure. Love is the greatest concept we can ever embrace. It is beautiful and is of God, for God is love.

Reflection

1) When in your life have you felt the most loved? By whom?

2) How have you experienced God's love for you?

3) Do you ever love with an if/then kind of love? Give an example.

4) When has someone loved you with an even/though kind of love?

5) Who in your life have you given an even/though forgiving love?

6) When you think of Jesus' crucifixion, what does it mean to you?

7) When you think of the empty tomb, how do you feel?

8) What benefit do you receive when you forgive someone?

9) How could our society benefit from a greater participation in generous love?

10) What one way this coming week can you better demonstrate Christlike loving and to whom?

TWO

Love's Prominence

In one of his plays, Jean Anouilh gave an intriguing description of the last judgment. I will paraphrase it:

At the gates of heaven, we find the good people compacted together like fans eager to enter the ballpark for an important game. They are sure that their reserved seats are among the very best. Saint Impatience surges through their bodies as they feel the push of the masses behind.

From nowhere a rumor makes its way through the crowd: "He's going to also forgive those others."

"Do you mean him too?"

"Not her! I can't believe it."

The look of disbelief engulfs their faces as sounds of disappointment mixed with anger are heard. "But I went to church nearly every Sunday and gave an extra amount to the building program!"

"If only I had known this, I would have...."

"God must be kidding; this must be some kind of joke."

The noise level of the angry crowd increases until they work themselves into a furious frenzy and start cursing God. They are all condemned at that very instant. This was their final judgment, and they prevented themselves from entering heaven.

Confronted with God's love, they refused to accept it for their brother and sister. "We can't approve of heaven for every Tom, Dick, and Harry."

"How can we love a God who loves so unconditionally? We are the good people; isn't heaven for the good people?"

God's love is as surprising as it is inclusive. Even the crowd which crucified Christ and the thief who shared his fate were objects of his love and forgiveness. Only a life in which God is not present would exclude Tom, Dick, and Harry.

God says that whatever does not spring from a heart full of love, however wonderful it may appear to others, counts as nothing. Pure love must be prominent in what we do if it is to be pleasing to the Lord. Everything worthwhile is grounded in love. To underline this most important point, Saint Paul gives several examples of commendable behavior. He then states emphatically that if they are devoid of love, they count for nothing.

Speaking In Tongues Without Love Is Just Noise

"If I speak in the tongues of mortals and angels, but do have not love, I am a noisy gong or a clanging cymbal" (1 Corinthians 13:1). Some of God's gifts are more dramatic and attention-getting than others. Speaking in tongues is one of them. Eloquent speech is another. In the early church these were coveted gifts.

"Tongues of mortals" here refers to the non-intelligible, ecstatic worship and praise that is prompted by the Holy Spirit. Generally, a feeling of great joy and of being filled with the presence of God accompanies this outpouring of praise. Unfortunately, like every other gift from God, this gift is given by a perfect God to an imperfect humanity.

Therefore, its use can range from an uninhibited, beautiful expression of praise of God to a self-indulgent desire to call prideful attention to oneself and one's religiosity. Love is the key that makes the difference. What's in the heart of the person who is speaking in tongues determines whether the praise demonstrates love for God or a behavior that is just calling attention to itself.

"Tongues... of angels" to which Saint Paul refers, most likely refers to the gift of eloquent speech. Look at Reagan, Churchill, Lincoln, and other noted speakers in history to see how powerful a gift eloquent speech is. Skilled use of this gift can inspire people to act; it can calm or arouse; it can move people and whole nations onto pathways of righteousness or onto roads of destruction. It can evoke both the noblest as well as the most depraved passions of the human spirit. Even so, eloquent speech from a Christian caught up in a love affair with self rather than with the Lord has little value in the church. Saint Paul declares that eloquent speech, along with speaking in tongues, can become as inconsequential as the gong and cymbal struck during parts of the worship service in the temple. On the other hand, when the love of Christ controls our hearts and directs our tongues, both in the praise and in the proclamation of the faith, these give glory to God and are valuable in the life of the church. Godly love gives of itself and does not seek to draw attention to itself. Benjamin Franklin put it another way, "Persons in love with themselves quickly discover they have no rivals."

Mountain Moving Faith Without Love
Is Worth Nothing

Sometimes, we are all a little thickheaded; so Saint Paul makes an even stronger statement for the superiority of love over all else. "And if I have prophetic powers, and understand all mysteries and all knowledge, and if I have all faith, so as to remove mountains, but do not have love, I am nothing" (1 Corinthians 13:2).

Saint Paul has no small regard for the gift of prophecy. He is not talking about the Old Testament kind of prophecy which was seen as predictive of the coming of Christ and his life and death. Rather, it involves the special gift of insight into things spiritual as well as a keen understanding of the mysteries of our faith. Seldom is prophecy criticized or even questioned in scripture. Nevertheless, here we are told that prophecy without love is worthless. Up against love, even highly esteemed prophecy pales. The greatest gifts of God given to individuals all become insignificant and useless when they do not emanate from a loving heart.

Knowledge has been revered in every age. Great thinkers and theologians have always been held in esteem, especially those we have deemed orthodox. Nevertheless, those who are gifted with special knowledge as well as those who hold to the correct understanding and teaching of the faith are warned by God's Word that knowledge must always be rooted in love.

We rarely win erring persons back to the truth by defeating them in an argument employing our superior knowledge. Even if they are big enough to see their mistake and acknowledge it, a loveless approach will not motivate an aberrant brother or sister to want to embrace a truth which was espoused by an opponent devoid of love. Certainly we must speak the truth to one another, but we must speak the truth in love.

Saint Paul, who has given us a greater understanding and appreciation of the importance of faith in our relationship to God than any other biblical writer, now says something most interesting: "And if I have all faith, so as to remove mountains, but do not have love, I am nothing." (1 Corinthians 13:2). He states that all faith, even the miracle working and mountain moving kind, is nothing unless based on love. Where there is no love, there is nothing we can do that pleases God.

Years ago, I attended an excellent evangelism seminar. The presenter was truly an inspiration and a great communicator of the faith. One could hardly imagine a non-believer resisting Christ once confronted by the truth so expertly delivered by this Christian gentleman. During the seminar, he confessed to us that as often as he tried to share his faith with his unbelieving father, he was always unsuccessful. He related, "We talked for hours, and I gave a clear testimony of my love for the Lord and explained the way of salvation to him." Why had he failed in sharing his faith with his father? Certainly he was a man of knowledge. Certainly he was eloquent. Certainly he was a man of faith. But just as certainly something was lacking in his relationship and witness to his dad.

"One day it came to me," he told us, "I had not been loving my father unconditionally. My love was conditioned on my father's response to my faith. After a long struggle capped by defeat, I learned that I first had to accept my father and love him whether or not he would ever come to Christ. I had to love him as a child of God — one whom the Father loves even in his unbelief. I simply stopped witnessing to him and started loving him as he was, I loved him uncritically and unconditionally. Touched not only with my love but also with God's love through me, my father soon accepted Jesus Christ as his Lord and Savior." Faith and knowledge without love is nothing.

Without Love, There Is No Gain in Giving Up Everything

"If I give away all my possessions, and if I hand over my body to be burned, but do not have love, I gain nothing" (1 Corinthians 13:3). Certainly, Jesus set his lasting seal of approval on generous benevolence. The Lord commanded the rich young ruler to sell all he had and give it to the poor. He commanded the disciples to turn their backs on their fishing business and follow him. Giving to the poor unselfishly is one of the loftiest of Christian virtues. Whenever we welcome a stranger in our house, clothe the naked, feed the hungry, or visit the sick and those in prison, Jesus commends such behavior. Saint Paul also encourages charity, saying that our giving must not only be marked by generosity but also by cheerfulness. As wonderful as philanthropy is, it must not be separated from love, or it too becomes nothing in God's eyes. True giving springs from a loving heart. It is godlike, for God so loved the world that he gave the greatest gift of all gifts to humankind, Jesus Christ.

In a church where I had served for many years, one of the Sunday school envelopes was opened by our counters only to discover there was no money in it. Nevertheless, the child who placed it in the offering plate that morning made perhaps the most pleasing offering of anyone present that day. In the envelope was a small piece of paper. On it was drawn a cross...the symbol of God's unconditional love. These words were also written on the paper, "Please forgive me, I have nothing to give but love." To have Christian love is not to have *nothing* but to have *everything*. It is the most important thing we can give to another.

Giving, even generous giving, can spring just as readily from the need for self-glorification as from a heart motivated by love. Loveless giving is often marked by the spirit of ostentation. The purpose of the giving is not primarily to feed the poor but bring glory and praise to the giver. Loveless giving in God's eyes is as useless as a boat in a desert.

Jesus castigated the baser sort of religious leader who chose the most prominent place in which to say prayers and give alms. The loveless giver would even have a trumpet blown to attract a crowd. The larger ostentatious donations commanded the attention and the respect of the temple crowds. Jesus, on the other hand, praised the widow who gave but a little mite. This gift went unnoticed by all but the discerning look of the Lord. She gave all she had. A large gift given without love ranks small in the sight of God. A small, insignificant gift given in love was viewed by Jesus as indeed great.

Once someone came into my church office and made a $1,000 donation to the church. The donor had never been so generous in the past. He told me, "Pastor, I thought I had better do this. I just had a serious financial loss. I know when you are generous with God, he is generous with you. I did not think I could afford not to make this donation." Here was a generous gift that did not emanate out of love but out of greed. Local government officials are never so willing to be helpful to the average citizen than before upcoming elections. The streets in the town are swept clean, and the grass is cut regularly. Passing town employees on the street fixing something, you are surprised that everyone seems to be actually working. What appears to be good service to the community unfortunately is motivated by the selfish desire to be reelected.

Years ago, the parish I served decided to expand its facilities at a projected expense of over a million dollars. At the time, this was a very large amount. Although the parish was large, it was still a formidable challenge.

During our campaign to secure gifts and pledges to the building fund, I had several sleepless nights and times of self-doubt. "How could we ever reach so high a goal?" I worried. Generous three-year pledges began to be made by many. Such an outpouring of generosity certainly helped to assuage my doubt. But it still lingered.

On the desk in my church office sat an old cast iron bank in the shape of a church. It had been used for years in the Sunday school. I had recently used it for a children's devotion. Periodically during the expansion fund raising campaign, children would walk into my office and place a few nickels and pennies into it. I never encouraged it. They simply did this on their own.

One day, a little third-grader came waltzing into my office smiling from ear to ear. "Pastor, I have something for God and for the expansion," she said happily. She then took a half-dollar piece out of her little purse. "This is my favorite coin," she announced with a smile. And before I could say anything, it went clinking into the church-shaped bank.

I was deeply touched by her generosity motivated by love. "Honey, your beautiful gift is going to build our new building which will help us serve the Lord better," I told her.

Tears filled my eyes — for the Lord had sent one of his angels into my office. Her love touched me deeply and pulled me from the powerful clutches of fear that breeds defeat. We had the most successful financial campaign in the 125 year history of the parish. In three months' time, our entire congregation effectively increased its giving by 50%. A fifty-cent piece — a child's mite given with love — was the impetus which led us to success. Love is powerful stuff.

Even Martyrdom Without Love Gains Nothing

"And if I hand over my body to be burned, but do not have love, I gain nothing" (1 Corinthians 13:3). Not even martyrdom is always pure. Self-glorification is possible even here. The true martyr does not seek his cross any more than Jesus sought his. But when a martyr is called upon to bear the cross for the sake of the faith, the cross is to be embraced and endured out of love. Using the extremity of martyrdom as his illustration, Saint Paul powerfully drives home his point that it is love that gives Christlike validity to our actions. If love for Christ and for our brothers and sisters is lacking, then not even a martyr's death brings about gain.

Saint Paul makes his message crystal clear. Love is not only the more excellent way to a successful life, but it is the most prominent virtue in scripture from which all God-pleasing activity must flow. There is nothing like love. It does not take second place to anything.

Reflection

1) What are your favorite love songs?

2) Have you ever experienced someone speaking in tongues or giving a prophecy? What are your thoughts about these kinds of gifts of the Spirit?

3) If someone like Adolf Hitler makes it to heaven having somehow confessed his sins to God before he died, how would you feel spending eternity with him?

4) If you do a good deed and then look for thanks or praise, does such a desire for recognition lessen the possibility that love was the motivating factor?

5) If love is the greatest virtue in God's eyes, what do you feel is second?

6) What really is love in your opinion and what all does it encompass?

7) Is it wrong to love yourself?

8) Why do you think that love is even held in higher esteem than faith?

9) How does the Lord's love for you encourage your love for others?

10) What special act of love would you be willing to do this week?

THREE

Love Is Patient And Kind

"Are you saying that Christ was a man and did not sin?"

"Yes, he was the only man who ever lived a perfect life."

"I can't believe that; it would be as easy for me to believe that as it would for me to believe I could put my fist through that cinder block wall behind your desk."

Other than the grunt I received when I welcomed him at the door of my office for the first class of my new members' course, this had been my only conversation with Steve. He and his wife, who was already a member of our church, came to the first class. She introduced him to me, "This is my husband Steve; he's Jewish." Then she left.

Throughout the class, Steve looked bored and disgruntled. Up until he questioned the sinless nature of Christ, he sat quietly with that look on his face. No one had ever before questioned the sinless nature of Christ in one of my classes. I answered him, "Christ was the Son of God and was perfect in every way. Because of this, he was able to pay the price of our sinfulness on the cross." It was easy to see that Steve wasn't buying it. At the end of the class, I asked everyone to bow their heads for a prayer. Steve didn't.

Honestly, there was a side of me that hoped Steve wouldn't show up for the second class. He was disruptive and gruff. I rationalized my feelings, thinking that it would be better for the others in the class without him. Steve came to the second class. My patience was stretched. At the end of the third class, Steve made a startling statement. "The other night, I was lying in bed talking to God. I don't know how to pray, so I just talk to God. I said 'God, I have a son, and my son is a lot like me. I believe you are perfect, God' — and then it hit me," Steve continued. "God's Son could well be just like him, perfect. Yes, I guess I could believe that Jesus was sinless like his father," Steve concluded. A breakthrough was beginning to occur.

When we got to the lesson on baptism, Steve became concerned. "You mean, if I want to be a Christian, I must be baptized?" he queried.

"Yes," I replied.

"I'm not sure I really believe," Steve continued. "I didn't grow up in Christianity, never went to Sunday school, and know very little about it."

"Steve, I'd love for you to be baptized — but don't do it because I want it for you or your wife wants you to. When you believe in Jesus Christ as your Lord and Savior, then you should be baptized and become a Christian."

Steve completed the course and wasn't baptized. In the next few months, he periodically came into my office and asked questions about the faith. His search continued. I needed to be patient with both Steve and God. I had to trust that God loved Steve immensely and was working to claim him as a child through baptism.

Then one afternoon Steve burst into my office and proclaimed, "I want to be baptized!"

"Great," I responded. "Why?"

"Because I accept Jesus as my Lord," Steve said with conviction. Then he related what happened on a recent hunting trip. "This past week, my father-in-law and I were in the Adirondacks deer hunting. We worked out a signal of firing a couple of shots in the air in order to keep track of one another. I had been hunting for some time and decided to check in with him. I fired off the signal shots. He did not respond. Again I fired. No response. All of a sudden it hit me that I was lost. What an awful feeling to be lost in the woods. Fear seized me, and I began to pray out loud to the Lord: 'God, this is Steve. I'm lost; I'm scared, too. I need your help to get me out of here.'"

Then Steve told me that he felt led to turn right followed by another course correction — and within minutes, he came to a road and was out of the woods and safe. "Pastor," Steve continued, "all these months I have been looking for a sign, and this was my sign. Some people may say it was a coincidence, but I firmly believe it was my sign."

I will never forget Steve's baptism. As he stood before the congregation, I asked him, "Do you believe in Jesus Christ as your Lord and Savior? If so then respond, 'Yes, with the help of God.'"

"Absolutely!" Steve responded loudly and with great conviction.

Steve moved to another state. Yet, every Christmas morning for years, I thought of him. Soon after his baptism, Steve and I talked about Christmas traditions in our homes. Steve told me that every Christmas his family enjoyed lox and bagels with cream cheese and raw onion. This is something especially enjoyed by Jewish people. We tried it for the first time. Ever since, it has been a favorite of ours — especially on Christmas morning. It also helps my family celebrate the Bethlehem birth of a very special Jewish boy.

"Love is patient; love is kind," (1 Corinthians 13:4). Saint Paul writes. Steve certainly gave our entire new member class a great opportunity to practice patience and kindness. One member of the class, Peter, befriended the irascible Steve and met with him sharing his faith and love. It was the good news of God's patient and kind love reaching out to Steve that prepared him for his special sign delivered during a hunting trip. And to think that I had silently hoped that Steve would not return after the first class! I am thankful God is also patient with me.

In the next few verses of his love poem, Saint Paul concretely tells us how Christian love works. Using crisp adjectives and action verbs, he describes love in all its beauty and possibility. Those of us who are wise enough to welcome love into our lives with all its power and nuances will be granted a more joyous and peaceful life. Patience is a virtue we appreciate in those who surround us. "Be patient, God is not finished with me yet," reads a popular poster. Having been a recipient of patient love many times in my life, I can attest that it is a beautiful gift to receive.

Love Is Patient And Magnanimous

Our God has been the supreme example of patient love. The translators of the King James Version of the Bible wrote, "Love suffereth long" (1 Corinthians 13:4). Patient love is long-suffering love. Once again, God's long-suffering love for the children of Israel — as well as for us — readily comes to mind. It is amazing how well God keeps righteous anger under control. The Bible is a story of God's patience from Abraham to Jesus Christ. God is patiently long-tempered. God endures the weakness of humankind. God has patience with a purpose — and that purpose is that all shall be saved.

The people of Corinth, with whom Saint Paul visited, were often difficult people to love. Their uncouth ways would regularly step on the sensitivities of tender feelings. To nurse a grievance, retaliate in kind, or even resent them could have resulted so naturally. Loving them with patience and kindness became a special challenge for Saint Paul and other faithful Christians. Perhaps the word *magnanimous* is helpful in expressing what Saint Paul is encouraging. We must be magnanimous in our loving of one another. While we were sinners, Jesus Christ died for us; his love was magnanimous. Patience and kindness are aspects of magnanimous love.

Jesus entreats us to love magnanimously. He calls upon us to forgive our enemies, love those who hate our guts, pray for those who drag our name through the mud, and walk the second mile with those who make unreasonable demands. "God, this takes great patience and kindness," we can easily protest. "I know all about it, for you test my patience and kindness all the time," God responds.

Patient love is also characterized by tenderheartedness and endurance. You can learn many things from a child, like how much patience you have. Our patience suffers quietly as a parent tries to comfort a cranky child during a worship service. Sitting in the fourth pew from the front of a large church I visited one Sunday, I observed a young mother trying to control her three-year-old. The young assistant pastor of the church struggled to deliver his message over the considerable commotion the child was creating. My attention was drawn from the sermon to the unruly child. Soon, I discovered the little one had to go to the bathroom. The mother encouraged her to wait; the child would have none of it and became upset.

I felt sorry for the poor young mother. "Her old man was probably home in bed." I thought. I also felt bad for the pastor who was trying to get his message across. I even felt compassion for the child who had to go to the bathroom.

Children have little patience in these fundamental matters. Finally, when all else had failed, the mother got up and walked her daughter down the very long aisle of the church as the child screamed, "I've got to pee-pee; I've got to pee-pee!"

Leaving the church after the service, I overheard many of the congregation commenting on the disruptiveness of the child. But instead of being irritated, they seemed surprisingly amused, and some appeared even pleased by the event. I came to find out that the screaming child was the young preacher's kid. On this Sunday, the parishioners all felt healed from all of the times their own children had embarrassed them in church. Love is patient and long-suffering with crying babies as well as with all of God's children.

Patience also suffers with teenagers, too, when they are hanging with the wrong group. Patience suffers long through a spouse's mid-life crisis because love is stronger than the crisis. Patience bites its tongue at your church's congregational meeting when others are speaking just to be heard. Love is patient, tenacious, long-suffering and does not easily give up on someone. We are an imperfect people dealing with other imperfect people. A greater measure of patient love will provide a greater measure of happiness in our lives and in the lives of others around us. Patient love also acquires fewer enemies.

Love Is Abundantly Kind

As stated earlier, to be patient is to be long suffering like Christ and to be able to practice self-restraint. To be kind is a more active expression of our love for others. Love that is patient most often also reveals itself in kindness.

One of my friends asked me to pray for her boss. "He is such an unhappy and unkind person; pray for him, pastor," she pleaded with me. "He made my entire week miserable." We all have received scars from people who have treated us unkindly. More often than we care to admit, our words and actions have also added to the unkindly spirit so prevalent in our world. But what are the characteristics of a kind person? They are friendly and generous and gentle. They are persons who are sympathetic and who have a warm-hearted nature. They are benevolent and caring. Christian love exhibits all of these fine qualities. On the outdoor bulletin board of the local Methodist church, I once read, "Kindness is never wasted." Whether or not that statement is true in every instance, it certainly encourages us to be more generous with our kindly acts. My high school math teacher ended each class by saying, "Make it a better day for someone else." We can make it a better day for someone else by touching them with our loving kindness.

It is not hard to call to mind the kindness God has lavished on all of us. His mercy is so abundant. Jesus' life exhibited abundant kindness. He stood up for a prostitute. He took pity on the ill man who laid at the pool of Bethesda. He called to himself the pesky children the disciples tried to keep away. On Calvary's cross, peering through pain, Jesus asked Saint John to care for his mother even as his own life ebbed away. These are but a few of many examples which grace the pages of scripture.

Loving-kindness gives the other person the benefit of the doubt. When we have every cause to blast someone with our self-righteous anger, loving-kindness prevents us from doing so. Consider also those times we justly deserve the full force of someone's ire for something thoughtless we did. Isn't it wonderful when that person instead treats us kindly by enduring our sin and forgiving us? Such love directed our way causes us to be more mindful of our wrongdoing and to desire to never do it again. Anger elicits more anger in return. Kindness elicits the desired response of changed behavior. Kindness is seldom if ever wasted.

Love's kindness finds the less fortunate as a frequent object of our attention. It looks for opportunities to do helpful acts. Sure, random acts of kindness are good — but regular acts of kindness are the ideal. To become Christ's hands of caring for the less fortunate becomes our goal. God's compassionate work in the world needs our hands to carry it out. When we pray for the less fortunate, God answers our prayers by inspiring us to become involved in alleviating their pain. Kindness respects all humankind regardless of race, creed, or class. Even when someone is clearly wrong, kindness accepts their right to be wrong. It recognizes that every person is fighting some kind of tough battle in their life. They are not always at their best. Kindness allows for that. Kindness is one of the most convincing signs of Christian love and acceptance.

I made a big mistake during the contentious 2016 presidential election. On Facebook, someone posted parts of a speech by one senator who took one of the candidates to task. Agreeing with much of what was said, I decided to hit the "Share" option. Every reaction — both good and bad — was posted for months on my Facebook page. There were nearly a thousand. I opened only a few. Some thoughtfully agreed with the post and others didn't. But what was amazing and alarming was the hate that spewed forth from many who commented. Not only was the senator attacked, but I was attacked as well. One recent post read, "Your an idiot!" I felt like replying, "It's 'You're an idiot,' idiot" But I was writing this book at the time and thought better of it. Instead, I replied, "It's 'You're an idiot.' God bless you, my fellow American — Pastor Krahn." While this was better than my first instinct, I probably should have only sent the second line of my reply.

True lovingkindness is uncalculating. It gives of itself without any expectation of a return on its investment. One person quipped that a good test of our generous kindness comes when the offering plate is passed, and we look in our wallet and only find a hundred dollar bill there. Kindness purchases the unneeded products kids sell at our door. Kindness refrains from blowing the car horn even when the jerk in front of you really deserves it. Kindness tries to find something good to say about someone who really makes such speech difficult.

A minister was busy in his study preparing his sermon for the coming Sunday. He reached for a book, then remembered he left it downstairs. He called his little daughter to fetch it for him while explaining carefully where she would find it. She went gladly and returned in a moment with a book which he quickly recognized was the wrong one. Taking the book from her, he kissed his daughter and said, "Thank you, sweetheart, for being so helpful to Daddy." With a big smile on her face, she skipped out of her father's study. The minister then went quietly and retrieved the book he needed. This is kindness.

An elderly lady went to the post office and discovered a workman busy installing some kind of machine. She discovered it was the latest stamp machine. He encouraged her not to wait in line for purchasing stamps. Eyeing the machine, she asked the workman a most important question: "Tell me, will the machine ask me about my rheumatism?" Unfortunately, only humans can dispense kindness.

In the classic comic strip "Tiger," a little boy stands and watches a little girl carry a football right past him. When criticized by his teammates for not tackling her, he said, "I was afraid I'd hurt her." The last frame of the comic strip shows him on his way home saying, "I got thrown out of the game for unnecessary gentleness." Gentleness is the twin sister of kindness.

We see kindness when a husband gives his terminally ill wife an expensive gift she is unlikely to ever wear. Kindness is confronting a smelly street person, and without being asked, handing him a ten-dollar bill saying, "Excuse me sir, I think you may have dropped this." Kindness is catching a person in an embarrassing situation and acting as though you did not see or hear what caused the embarrassment.

One of the most beautiful acts of kindness done by members of my former congregation was to provide a *Love Feast* for families who suffered the death of a loved one. With the family's permission, while the family is at the cemetery, members of the parish come to their home and set up a full meal for 25 people. Everything is provided, down to paper plates and napkins. When the grieving family returns home, all is prepared. Those who prepared the meal leave before they return. It is like a miracle. It is the miracle of lovingkindness. Along with the delicious meal, they enjoy this beautiful act of kindness.

Kids Define Kindness

Children often have special insights into things. I asked some of the third graders and sixth graders in a Lutheran school to write and complete the sentence "Kindness is..." Here are some of the writings of the third graders:

"Kindness is when I did something bad, and my brother did not tell on me."

"Kindness is when someone breaks something that is important to you, and you don't get angry at them."

"Kindness is giving food and money to others and not just to brag but because you wanted to."

Sixth graders had this to say: "When a friend was sleeping over, we were painting our nails on my new bed cover. When we were painting our nails, fluorescent green nail polish spilled on my cover. When my mom came into my room, she saw me trying to get it off and me crying and filled with fear. My mom told me that it was all right, and that I shouldn't get upset, and that she understood that I didn't mean to do it. This was kindness and love to me."

"Kindness is loading and unloading the dishwasher if your mother is pregnant."

"Kindness is just telling someone that his clothes look nice, or she is very pretty. It can change someone's whole day."

"Kindness is giving someone something if they need it more than you."

Most acts of kindness cost very little if any money. Yes, kindness often takes some effort — but nothing worthwhile is ever accomplished without effort. We must seek to always let our good deeds exceed our pious talk. The greater the obstacle someone puts in our way to loving them, the greater the joy we will experience when we finally overcome it. Patience and kindness are part of the more excellent way that makes love great.

Reflection

1) How is your patience tested the most?

2) Like in the story of Steve, with whom in your life have you had to be patient, and what was the outcome?

3) In your life, how were you blessed by receiving patient love from someone else?

4) How has God shown patience with you?

5) Who specifically needs magnanimous patient love from you?

6) Who in your life was a model of a kindly person and why?

7) When have you especially felt the need for kindness in your life?

8) How do you exhibit loving kindness in your life?

9) At the end of this chapter, which one of the children's definitions of kindness especially spoke to you? Why?

10) Who this week needs some special kindly love from you?

FOUR

Love Is Not Envious Or Boastful

At eight-years old, my younger daughter decided to make her first attempt at negotiating a raise in her allowance. She eagerly presented her well-thought- out case for an increase of a dollar per week. I listened in amused silence.

Having agreed in my mind to the proposed increase, I decided to give her two alternatives from which to choose. I would either give her and her sister the dollar increase she requested, or I would raise her allowance two dollars and her older sister's four dollars. "It is your choice — one dollar each or two for you and four more for your sister," I told her.

Although my second alternative would have provided her twice what she had initially requested, she could not live with the thought that her sister would receive four dollars to her two. She accepted the dollar she initially proposed and said that would make her happy. In her mind, this was fair and the other wasn't.

Perhaps a sense of fairness motivated her decision. If she were the recipient of the four dollars and her sister the two dollars, I wondered if the issue of fairness would have been quite so compelling.

But how about us as adults? Would we be happier receiving a thousand dollar raise along with a co-worker who does the same job as we do, or would we be happier receiving two thousand while our co-worker gets four thousand? If given the choice, we may be wise enough to take the two thousand, but many of us would be unhappy receiving the two thousand when our co-worker got four. Why? Much of the reason, I believe, can be attributed to the sin of envy.

45

We would be unhappy and envious of our co-worker's better treatment. Saint Paul writes, "Love is not envious" (1 Corinthians 13:4).

Envy Is The Enemy Of Love

A terrible old joke goes, "Why did Cain kill his brother?" The answer, "Because he was Abel." The correct answer is, "Because he was angry and envious." God accepted Abel's sacrifice but not Cain's. In a jealous rage, he killed his brother. Envy caused the first crime recorded in scripture. The Bible is full of examples of envy. Rachel is envious of Leah's ability to bear children when she could not. Joseph was sold into slavery because of the envy of his brothers. Envy over David's success leads to the downfall of King Saul. The older brother in the parable of the prodigal son was envious of the party the father threw for his rogue brother upon his return home. King Solomon rightly remarked that, "For jealousy arouses a husband's fury, and he shows no restraint when he takes revenge" (Proverbs 6:34). Saint James writes, "For where there is envy and selfish ambition, there will also be disorder and wickedness of every kind" (James 3:16).

In the Bible, envy is seen as an emotion of single-minded devotion. When our devotion focuses only upon ourselves, we do not see the needs of others. Rather, be envious for the well-being of others — a devotion not centered on ourselves but on others. This moves us from selfishness to selflessness. The difference can be seen in two propositions: to be envious *of* someone can lead to sin; to be envious *for* the good of another can lead to behavior that pleases God. Saint Paul speaks of the former when he writes, "Love is not envious or boastful"(1 Corinthians 13:4). Love is not self-seeking or self-promoting but seeks the welfare and praise of others before itself.

Envy poisons personal relationships. Although all of us are equal in God's sight, we are not equal in God-given ability. Some people are also born into more influential families

46

which give them the opportunity to achieve the better things in life. The owner's son or daughter has a big leg up in becoming an executive in their parent's company. At several wedding receptions I have attended over my long career, the lead singer was far superior to a singer I had recently heard on a late-night television show. Being at the right place at the right time has a lot to do with success. Have we not all felt the pangs of envy as we considered those whom we feel to be more splendidly gifted, better looking, or perhaps just lucky to be at the right place at the right time?

As they were growing up, my children had an obsession with fairness as I earlier alluded. Everything I did for one had to be done in equal measure for the other. If one got one more M&M than the other, protest would immediately follow, "She got six M&Ms and I only got five!" Most kids are like that. For years, I was almost obsessed with proving to my children that I loved them both the same. In all things, I endeavored to be fair. Finally, one day when I was being reprimanded for unfairness, in frustration I stated, "You are right, I was unfair. From now on I will not treat you both equally." My accusing daughter looked at me in shocked disbelief." I continued, "You are both different, and it is impossible for me to treat you equally in all things." Life is like that. It is unequal and, at times, unfair. Feelings of unfairness come when we perceive that we are getting less than we think we deserve. And it is also unfair when we receive more than we deserve. But we rarely protest that.

God calls forth from us a love that is magnanimous. As hard as it might be, we are to rejoice when we receive a $2,000 raise even while our co-worker gets a $4,000 raise. When we lose in a sport, we need not be envious of our opponent's success.

Like an infected wound, the sin of envy spreads. It breeds hatred that leads to strife. Only Christian love is strong enough to endure the difference in social status, God-given gifts and abilities, and circumstances that are part of every life. For, life is not fair. It is not equal. When our envy causes us to lament, "Poor me," nothing good comes out of it.

Envy is an enemy within and stays with us wherever we go. It constantly eats away at us. However much we have, however many breaks come our way, however good our life is; envy seeks to find someone who has it better. It focuses on what we don't have rather than on the abundance we already possess. Our happiness and wellbeing are lessened by envy. Relationships are prevented from reaching their full potential because of it. If left unchecked, it can even lead to tragedy.

A Greek legend relates the story of a runner who is envious of an opponent who beats him in every race. Finally, a statue is erected honoring his opponent.

Filled with envy, the defeated man vows to destroy the statue. Every night, unseen, he quietly chisels away at the base of the statue. Night after night, he continues undetected. One night he finally succeeds and the statue falls. But it falls on him and kills him. Was it the statue that killed him or was it envy?

When envy rampages through us, perhaps it is symptomatic of a far deeper spiritual problem. Most of our envy emanates from a life which puts far too much emphasis on things that are material rather than spiritual. We do not have to consult our bank balance to discover our wealth. Rather, we should consider the cross and the empty tomb as a measure of the wealth of forgiveness and an eternal future which is ours. Our lives need to focus on the eternal rather than on the temporal. Envy is evidence of love out of focus. We cannot serve two masters, Jesus rightly tells us (Matthew 6:24; Luke 16:13).

"Love is not envious," (1 Corinthians 14:4), Saint Paul writes. Christian love fed by God's word and sacraments aggressively promotes the well-being of others. It centers its attention and goodwill on others and rejoices in the success of brothers and sisters. And when it does, all heaven rejoices. The greatest love is a love free of envy.

Love Does Not Blow Its Own Horn

A woodpecker is tapping away at a dead tree. As he works, the sky darkens and thunder is heard. Not missing a beat, he continues on working. It begins to rain. Tap... tap... tap... the woodpecker presses on. Suddenly, a huge bolt of lightning hits the tree. Not knowing what hit him, the woodpecker picks himself up off the ground, shakes his feathers, discovers he is all right, and observes the shattered tree. Taking flight, he begins shouting to every creature in the forest, "Come see what I did; come see what I did!"

"Love is not ...boastful," (1 Corinthians 14:4) Saint Paul writes. Our pride causes us to think more highly of ourselves than we should.

When we seek to lift ourselves up in everyone's eyes — to put ourselves high on a pedestal — our energies are being misdirected. The Bible cautions against human presumption and self-glorification. God alone is to be glorified and exalted. The great gospel hymn is "How Great Thou Art," not "See How Great I Am."

Jesus gives pride a leading place among the list of vices which need to be displaced by the spirit of Christian love. Whereas envy is an inward state of sin, boastfulness is an outward expression of an unchristian spirit. The person filled with God's love need not indulge in self-display. They realize that someone wrapped up in themselves makes a rather small package. When a person starts to sing their own praises, it is pretty certain to be a solo. Rather, the Christian filled with the spirit of love joins the chorus of others in the praising of others. There are many ways of manifesting pride, but love is incompatible with them all.

49

Have you noticed that really great people rarely boast of their accomplishments? Rather, they have an engaging atmosphere of quiet humility about them. They rarely indulge in self-aggrandizement. If there is something to boast about, others are left to sound the trumpet. Conceit is a strange illness that makes everyone sick except the person who has it. In defense of the boastful, a humorist once said, "At least an egotist never goes around talking about other people." Saint Paul, in 2 Corinthians, writes: "I will not boast except of my weaknesses... I will boast all the more gladly of my weaknesses, so that the power of Christ will dwell within me." People who are all caught up in themselves squeeze out room for God in their lives.

As a child, when I would begin to boast about something, my father said to me, "John, always remember, 'SPS.'" It stands for "Self... Praise... Stinks." He only had to tell me what these three little letters meant. From then on, he would say "SPS" when I needed to hear it. As you can see, he said it frequently enough during my childhood that I still remember it.

Humble Love Glorifies God

Sinful pride displaces God as first in our lives. It is hard to love God with all of our heart, mind, soul, and being when we are so busy loving ourselves. Now, all self-love is not sinful. It is loving one's self more than God that is sinful. It is praise of ourselves rather than acknowledging that all we are and have comes from a gracious God. God deserves all *praise, all honor, and all glory.* Sure we recognize our talents and abilities. We can feel good about them — but we recognize they are all gifts from God, from first to last. God does not want to see our pride hurt; God wants to see it killed. Pride gets in the way of a wholesome relationship with God. It can even cause spiritual death when we become so full of ourselves that there is no room left in our lives for God.

In Greek mythology, Icarus was taken prisoner along with his craftsman father. To escape, the father made wings of feathers and wax for both of them. As they flew away, the father warned his son not to fly too close to the sun, or his wings would melt and fall off. Having escaped, Icarus' bursting pride caused him to soar too high in the heavens until the sun melted his wings — and he fell into the sea and died. Pride kills not only mythological figures but we modern-day people as well.

How easily we can become like the crowing rooster. The rooster prays, "Do not forget, Lord, that it is I who makes the sun rise." "Being cocky," we call it. So often, we cannot see God's obvious hand in our lives. So if love is not cocky and boastful, what is it? Great love is humble. Saint Augustine brought more people to Christ through his humble life than through his brilliant theological works. As prodigious and great a genius as Johann Sebastian Bach was, he consistently signed his compositions with the phrase *Soli Deo Gloria* – "To God alone be the glory." Years ago, Clarence Jordan, a New Testament Greek scholar as well as a farmer, was extremely popular on the lecture circuit. Someone asked him whether the warm receptions he received did not spoil him. He replied that when he got home, he jumped up on the manure spreader and that brought him back to earth.

True love performs even the humblest of tasks. We think of Jesus washing the feet of his disciples and ask ourselves what possibly could be beneath our dignity. Saint Francis of Assisi once kissed a leper on the mouth to demonstrate his humble love for humankind. He knew God's love through Christ was so much more of a sacrifice. Christians who realize that every good and perfect gift is from above rarely get sore arms from patting themselves on the back. Rather, their arms get tired from constantly being raised in praise of God.

There is the story about a man who wished to be humble. He was very happy when he managed to be humble. But he was very sorry that he was happy that he was humble. And

51

he was very happy that he was so sorry that he was happy that he was humble ... and so there is no way out of this vicious circle. Martin Luther wrote that true humility does not know that it is humble — for if it did, it would be proud from contemplating so fine a virtue.

Humble love finds no one beneath its consideration. All humans are worthy objects of its respect. The smelly street person is as worthy an object of our love and respect as the company president, the famous citizen, the star, and our parents. Humble love includes. It is fully and gratefully aware that it was first included into the sphere of God's heavenly love and forgiveness. Acknowledging its debt before God, Christian love cannot boast except in the abundance of the grace of God. Love is not envious or boastful.

Reflection

1) Share a time when you felt really envious of someone.

2) How has either past or present feelings of envy affected your life negatively?

3) Share a time when you celebrated the good fortune of someone who received something you really desired and they received it instead of you.

4) What is the root cause of your feelings of envy and how might you overcome it?

5) Share something for which Christian love can be envious.

6) What things in your life makes you itch to boast about to others?

7) How does it feel being around people who are constantly boasting about their children, grandchildren, expensive purchases, accomplishments, etc.

8) Why is pride sinful?

9) If love is not boastful or proud, then what is it?

10) What can you rightfully boast about?

FIVE

Love Is Not Arrogant Or Rude

Have you ever been put down by someone and made to look foolish or stupid? At one time or another, this probably has happened to all of us. When I went away to prep school at thirteen-years old intending to study for the ministry, I was a fat child with a high-pitched voice and a Maryland accent. Coming to school in New York, I was an easy target for ridicule.

Although I have many fond memories of those years, I can vividly remember times of pain from being put down by classmates. Entering the ninth grade, I was a very poor student. As a matter of fact, the first marking period, I flunked religion. Can you believe it — going away to study for the holy ministry and flunking religion? During my first and second year in prep school, I often tasted the arrogance and rudeness of the unseemly side of classmates and upperclassmen. It tasted terrible. I hated it.

You too, I am sure, at times have had your spirit crushed by arrogance and rudeness directed your way.

Christian love is not arrogant or rude. On the positive side, we could say that Christian love exhibits good manners. It is not boorish. It neither has a swelled head nor a lethal tongue. It does not harbor inflated ideas of its own importance. It does not abuse others by words or deeds.

If anyone in human history had a good reason for being inflated with himself, it was our Lord Jesus Christ. Yet, throughout his entire ministry, we see example after example of gentleness in dealing with hurting people he encounters. Here are just two examples.

While Jesus was eating in Simon the Pharisee's house, a woman of the street came in uninvited and washed Jesus' feet with her tears and wiped them with her own hair. She then kissed his feet and anointed them with some costly ointment she had brought with her.

The Lord was then criticized for not having the prophetic insight to know that a loose woman was touching him. Instead of preserving his sense of dignity with arrogant self-righteousness by kicking the prostitute away from himself, he tenderly commended her acts of love. He even elevated her above his host by saying, "I entered your house, you gave me no water for my feet, but she has bathed my feet with her tears and dried them with her hair. You gave me no kiss, but from the time I came in, she has not stopped kissing my feet. You did not anoint my head with oil, but she has anointed my feet with ointment" (Luke 7:44-46). Can you imagine the look on everyone's face?

Then, to cap it all off, Jesus forgave her sins! Only God forgives sins, and this rabbi, not yet known or accepted as the Messiah, forgave her sins. "Therefore, I tell you, her sins, which were many, have been forgiven; hence she has shown great love. But the one to whom little is forgiven, loves little. Then he said to her, 'Your sins are forgiven'" (Luke 7:47-48). The Lord's love is not only generous but gentle. No one was seen as being beneath him or out of the reach of his love. The depth of his love did not allow him to look down upon anyone or to put them down. It was blind to color, class, creed, or character. It simply saw people as those the Father loved.

People with needs, people with hurts, people with problems — sinful people needing salvation — were the ones that his love, devoid of arrogance and rudeness, chose to see and serve.

Love Washes Feet

The setting for the second example of Christ's giving and gentle love comes close to his death. On the night in which Jesus was betrayed, as he and his disciples gathered in the upper room, something seemed to be wrong. Although it is not explicitly stated in the narrative, we can surmise what it might have been. But first, let us set the stage a bit. In our Lord's time, when people gathered for a meal, it was the slave's duty to wash the feet of the guests as they reclined at the table. The Lord and his disciples were poor, and therefore without the services of a slave. The disciples probably took turns washing off the dust of the road from the sandaled feet of the little brotherhood. Normally, they did it willingly as a matter of course. But tonight, all of them sat stubbornly in their places and would have none of this menial task.

Perhaps, on their journey to the upper room, they continued to argue with one another about who would have the position of honor when Jesus ushered in the kingdom of God that he so frequently spoke about. Perhaps, with ruffled feathers and sore feelings, they trooped into the upper room like a set of sulking schoolboys — not one of them willing to see the pitcher of water and basin and towel set there for their use. For this once, the customary little courtesy was not carried out, and they began the Passover celebration with their feet still travel stained. An arrogant, uncompromising spirit prevailed.

Wanting to clear the air and cleanse this unseemly spirit out of their hearts, Jesus took the role of the servant, rose, and began to wash their feet. The disciples were shocked. Peter challenged the appropriateness of the Lord's action. In washing their feet, Jesus demonstrated his earlier words spoken just before he entered Jerusalem: "Whoever would be great among you must be your servant, and whoever would be first among you must be your slave; even as the Son of Man came not to be served but to serve and to give his life as a ransom for many." (Matthew 20: 26-28)

Arrogance and rudeness has no place in the Lord's service. Jesus did feet. When was the last time any of us washed another person's feet? Love that controls better-than-thou attitudes rolls up its sleeves and cleans dirty feet. Any act of kindness emanating from a heart filled with love which has also kept prideful arrogance in check is commended by God.

The church in Corinth to whom Saint Paul wrote his love treatise in many ways lacked class. During times of gathering together, there was unmannerly conduct. People were likely jumping up and interrupting each other during worship services. Arrogance invaded the hearts of some of those who were given special gifts by the Holy Spirit. Rudeness followed and hurt feelings resulted.

To these people in Corinth, Saint Paul wrote, "Love is not... arrogant or rude" (1Corinthians 13: 4-5). Loving each other with Christ-like love minimizes self- glorification with its accompanying rudeness. Accepting the company and kindness of a public sinner who washed his feet and who later humbly washes the feet of his disciples can only come from a love focused on giving itself in behalf of others.

The Ultimate Form Of Arrogance

Although all forms and expressions of arrogance need to be purged from our lives, there is one insidious form of arrogance that infects the hearts and minds of many Christians. Many of us do not even recognize it as arrogance. For some in the church, it may even be part of their belief system. Nevertheless, it is the ultimate form of arrogance. It is even rude, for it displays ignorance of the full scope of the gospel. What is this abomination? It is a belief or practice that rejects Christ's death and resurrection as being all-sufficient in providing for our salvation. But we protest that we believe in

58

Jesus Christ and the forgiveness of sins. Yet, some of us feel that we must also do something to merit salvation in addition to believing in Jesus Christ as our Lord and Savior.

In James Kennedy's book *Evangelism Explosion,* he suggested that we all answer two diagnostic questions. The first was, "If you were to die tonight, do you believe you would go to heaven?" The second was, "If you were to stand before God and he were to ask you, 'Why should I let you into my heaven?' what would you answer him?" Now take a moment to think about your answers to both questions before reading further. Stop. Do not read any further. Please answer these two questions. It is surprising just how many people are not entirely certain of their salvation. All too frequently, answers to the first diagnostic question go something like this: "I hope so." "No one can be entirely certain." "No, I am not sure." Here is a frequent response to the second diagnostic question: "If I stood before God and he asked me why he should allow me to come into his heaven, I'd say that I tried to lead a good life. I haven't gone out of my way to hurt anyone, and I have tried to be a good husband and father."

The truth is that salvation is a free gift and can in no way be merited by anything we do. That we believe we can in any way participate in our own salvation is pure arrogance. For us to think that some goodness of our own helps us gain heaven also suggests that Christ's suffering and death on Calvary's cross lacked something and was not good enough to pay the entire price for our sins. It is a slap in Jesus' face.

We can do nothing to add to the power and efficacy of the cross and the empty tomb. An alternative translation of Jesus' words from the cross, "It is finished" (John 19:30), reads: "The debt is paid in full." Jesus did everything that was needed. Ours is but a beggar's hand that reaches out to a gracious God and by faith receives forgiveness and acceptance and salvation.

God has accepted us totally, completely, and eternally, through faith in God's Son. The only thing that we can do is accept God's acceptance. In John's gospel, we read, "everyone who believes in him may not perish but may have eternal life" (John 3:16). It cannot be clearer or simpler. For us to think that we can add anything to God's gift of salvation is arrogant and rude.

Love Is Never Withheld

Having been so completely accepted by God's abundant love through Christ without any merit of our own, are we not also arrogant when we withhold our love and forgiveness from others? How can we who have not been excluded from God's love exclude someone from ours? Christ's love includes not excludes. It is easy to love someone who is lovable. Anyone can do that. It is easy to love someone who loves us in return. Anyone can do that as well. God didn't love us because we deserved it but because we needed it. Likewise, our love is not limited to those in our lives whom we feel deserve it.

It was only after Christ's death and resurrection that Simon Peter fully realized this. In the book of Acts, we read about Peter while he was staying in Joppa. One afternoon, he had a vision while he was on the rooftop praying. He saw a large sheet being lowered from heaven to earth by its four corners. In it were all kinds of animals, reptiles, and wild birds. A voice from heaven told Peter to get up, kill, and eat. He refused, claiming that he would never eat anything considered defiled or unclean. A voice spoke saying, "What God has made clean, you must not call profane" (Acts 10:15). After experiencing this vision three times, Peter pondered its meaning.

A few days earlier God had dispatched an angel to Cornelius, a Roman centurion. The angel told Cornelius that God had accepted his prayers. He had told Cornelius to send his servants to Peter to invite him to come and speak with him and his family. After the servants arrived in Joppa and related to Peter what had happened to Cornelius, Peter joined them and returned to Caesarea. Arriving at Cornelius' home, both men shared with one another their special experiences. Peter then realized that God loves and treats all humans — both Jews and Gentiles — the same. After sharing the good news of Christ's life, death, and resurrection with Cornelius and those gathered together, the Holy Spirit came down on all who were listening. Peter then baptized all of them in the name of Jesus Christ.

The church, even today, continues to struggle with the sin of arrogant exclusivity. There was a time when people of color were not welcomed in churches that whites attended. Whenever we are inclined to invite some class or race over another into our churches, then this sin rears its ugly head. Christ welcomes all people. His church must do the same. There are no right people or wrong people... Christ died for all people.

Today, most of our churches are open to everyone — but how about our hearts? Are they inclusive or exclusive? If we were to have a vision like Peter, who would God put in our sheet and command us to love and accept? God shows no partiality. Neither should we.

On Mother's Day at a small country church, it was the pastor's custom to give little gifts in honor of motherhood. "Would the oldest mother please come forward?" he urged. Smiling, one of the grand old ladies hobbled up and received her gift of recognition. "I'd like the newest mother to come up," the pastor continued. Right from the hospital, the young mother carrying her freshly minted baby walked up and received her gift.

Sitting by her mother watching all of this is a little four-year-old girl. She is getting concerned, for the pastor had but one present left, and she wanted so badly for her mother to receive it. The pastor spoke again, "Finally, would the mother with the most children please come forward? There was a buzz of chatter in the church — but it was quickly determined that eight was the winning number, and another lady came forward to receive her gift.

The four-year-old, visibly disappointed, turned lovingly to her mother to comfort her. With a voice audible throughout the church, she spoke, "Don't worry, mother — if he had asked for the fattest mother, you would have won." Great love seeks to include.

Once, in a large Bible class of over 100 people, I was speaking about how a loving spirit that should even include people we do not like. The class took place just before Christmas when people planned parties. My wife and I were having a Christmas party in our home the following week. With conviction, I said,

Wouldn't it be interesting and God pleasing if all of us invited the people we didn't like to our Christmas parties and celebrations this year? The pain in the butt next door would get an invitation. We'd invite the person at work who always knifes us in the back. Our guest list would then become an expression of our appreciation for God's love at Christmas. We would be loving with an inclusive love by also inviting those people we have grown to despise.

At the time I spoke these words, I momentarily forgot that many of the guests for my upcoming Christmas party were in my Bible class. Good naturedly, they came up to me after class and asked whether they were being invited as friends or as people who would stretch the boundaries of my inclusive love. I assured them that our party was more along the traditional lines.

Love Can Be Risky

Love that is not arrogant is often vulnerable. We must extend ourselves and our love to even the more unsavory types. We risk rejection if we reach out to someone with whom we have a difficult relationship. But not to reach out with love is also risky. We risk never being able to remove the pain of our separation from this person. We risk never being able to fully experience the beauty and specialness of this person. We risk not doing God's will in loving even those people hard to love. Love is vulnerable. Love takes risks.

Sometimes, it helps me by making a special project out of someone whom I find easy to dislike. There are irritating people in all of our lives. I make one or more of them my special project for a few months. I keep them in my daily prayers. I ask the Lord to love them through me. When I see them, I treat them as if they were my best friend. Praying the Lord's Prayer, I think of these people as I pray, "Forgive us our debts as we also have forgiven our debtors" (Matthew 6:12).

As I now interact with these folks, previous offenses and problems are treated as though they never occurred. Try it. It doesn't always work in restoring every relationship (though some do improve). But it has never made a problem relationship worse. To be honest, it has its moments of pleasure — especially when you observe some of the surprised and baffled looks that appear on your adversary's face. I'm not saying that this pleasure you experience is godly; I'm just saying there are even a few devilish rewards.

Saint Paul calls upon us to love with compassion and class. Love is not tactless. It is meek and strong at the same time. It is meek in that it recognizes all that it has graciously received through Christ, and it is strong in its willingness to accept and reach out to others. It is an honorable love which does not tire of elevating God and others above itself. It is a love that goes the distance. It is a love that does not even feel good when the office gossiper has laryngitis. Rather, it wishes the gossiper a quick recovery. It never puts someone down but eagerly looks until it finds something good to say about them. Love at its greatest is not arrogant or rude.

Reflection

1) Share a time when you were hurt by someone's arrogance or rudeness.

2) When we compare our lives with Christ's, why is there no room for us to be arrogant?

3) Share a time when you were treated well by someone when you did not deserve it.

4) Share a time when you treated someone with gentleness and forgiveness when they did not deserve it.

5) If you were to die tonight, do you believe you would go to heaven?

6) If God was to ask you why should he allow you into his heaven, what would you answer him?

7) How important is it to you being saved by Christ, and how does this impact your daily life?

8) What might you do to draw closer to Christ this week?

9) Whose feet might Christ be calling you to wash this week?

10) When you are tempted to be either arrogant or rude to someone, what can you do to love that person instead?

SIX

Love Does Not Insist On
Its Own Way

A boy was called upon to give blood to his younger brother because of a serious accident his brother just suffered. The older brother had to come to the hospital suddenly and was hurriedly prepared for the transfusion. His father drove the boy to the hospital, but being upset, the father failed to explain what a transfusion was. The boy donned the hospital garb, and then laid down beside his younger brother. The needle was inserted in his left arm as he watched his pallid brother lying unconscious beside him. He looked up at the doctor who was making the transfusion — and as seriously as a boy could say anything, he asked, "When do I croak, Doc?"

The boy knew nothing about transfusions, and since no one had told him that it would be a harmless experience, he had actually felt during the hurried trip to the hospital and the transfusion itself that he was being asked to give his life for his younger brother. That innocent question, "When do I croak, Doc?" revealed to everyone that he never questioned what he had been asked to do. The boy's mother wept when she heard his question, as did one of the nurses. Two others blinked their eyes and coughed. The doctor asked for a towel and wiped his eyes. Here was a beautiful example of love that did not insist on its own way but was totally unselfish.

In the Bible, there are countless numbers of selfish people. Numerous characters had a relationship with God but only wanted it on their own terms.

Jonah was one of them. In the beginning of the Old Testament book that bears his name, we read: "Now the word of the Lord came to Jonah, the son of Amittai, saying, 'Go at once to Nineveh, the great city, and cry out against it, for their wickedness has come up before me'" (Jonah 1:2). Jonah responded to God's command by hotfooting it for Joppa to catch a boat heading for Tarshish, which is in the opposite direction from Ninevah. Who of us cannot see himself or herself in "let's not get involved in this difficult mess" Jonah?

We really have to admire old Jonah's determination. So determined is Jonah to not get involved that when a mighty storm arose, he was asleep. And when the ship's captain awakened him, Jonah told the crew that the way to solve the problem of their ship sinking was to throw him overboard into the sea. Jonah was not to be let off so easily, for the Lord had arranged to have a specially equipped fish meet Jonah as he came over the side.

Jonah's determination not to get involved still has a lot of appeal among us today. Family frictions, an unchurched community, homeless people, unbelievers destined to hell, billions of bellies exploding with the pain of hunger... all Ninevehs that God is calling us to engage. Many times we too wish we could climb into a boat's hold, go to sleep, and avoid such problems. But God calls us to care, and caring takes time and a spirit of loving selflessness. God also demands involvement in a world full of problems and without guarantees. Here again is what makes Jonah so appealing and so much like us. When Jonah looked at the problems involved in proclaiming God's word to the people of Nineveh, he didn't react like some psychotic who thought two plus two equals five. No, he was like you and me. He was just a good healthy neurotic who knew that two plus two equals four but was overwhelmed by life.

But there's just no escape. God had a plan for Jonah's life, and sleeping in the hold of a ship going in the opposite direction made no difference. God raised a storm, provided Jonah with the short straw, and gave him lodging in a customized, big fish. Jonah had three days to think things over in most unusual surroundings. He also did a lot of praying before the fish vomited him up on dry land. And even before Jonah could clean himself up and dry out, there was the Lord again calling him to love and care enough for the people of Nineveh to go and share the Lord's word with them.

This time Jonah went — and the people of Nineveh listened, clothed themselves in sackcloth, and repented. Jonah found out the hard way that obeying God was better than insisting on his own way.

Saint Paul's description of Christian love as not insisting on its own way follows quite naturally from his earlier comments that love is not arrogant, boastful, or rude. Love gives of itself to others unselfishly, for it has first received so much already from the Father through the Son. One's selfless love becomes a thankful response to God as it seeks to become a better neighbor.

Love Is Not Self-Centered

Unfortunately, the persistent call to self-centeredness beckons to us in many ways. We find it in literature. The heroes in television and film drama are often power hungry and stop at nothing to get their way. The business world is rarely altruistic — but rather, strives in every way to beat the competition and get more, more, more and grow bigger, bigger, bigger.

We also see this in our religious life. Our prayers often do not extend very far beyond our personal needs and problems. Ours prayers are often superficial because we want to quickly return to whatever we were doing.

Even some of our popular hymns are a bit too self-centered. Rather than being so subjective, worship and prayer should most often sound an objective note concentrating our attention upon God as the main focus and object of our worship. Certainly, God does watch over us and is intensely interested in us — but we are not the center of his attention exclusive of the rest of humankind.

Some Sunday after I lead worship and as the parishioners leave church, I'd like to have the nerve to ask each of them: "Well, how did you do this morning?" As they leave worship, most are not evaluating how they did but how everyone else did. They are thinking whether or not they liked my sermon or whether the hymns were good, and whether the choir's anthem was stirring.

The more important issue is how they did. Did they sing the hymns with fervor? Did they concentrate on the prayers, listen to the lessons, and consider how the points of the sermon interacted with their lives? Did they express their love and thanksgiving to God? We do not so much come to church on Sunday but come to worship. Worship is about God, not about us. There is a pronounced difference between going to church and coming to worship.

Christian love does not seek its own advantage but rather is willing to give up its own gain for the benefit of the neighbor. For the sake of others, it is willing to give up even what it is rightly entitled. Everyone's needs become as important as one's own. When the satisfaction and security of another person becomes as important as our own, then this selfless quality of love exists in us. Love's arms are always open for others for if we close our arms and no one is embraced, then we are left holding only ourselves.

Every year of his life, Frank Gajowniczek, a former sergeant in the Polish army, visited Auschwitz and laid a wreath on the bunker where a Franciscan friar named Maximilian Kolbe died in his stead. In July 1941, a prisoner had escaped from the death camp. In retaliation, the Nazis followed their usual procedure of selecting ten prisoners at random to be starved to death. Gajowniczek was one of the unfortunate ones chosen. He cried out that he wanted to live and see his wife and children once again. Suddenly, Father Kolbe, who was in Gajowniczek's line, stepped forward. He told the commandant that he wanted to take the place of the man who had a family. An eyewitness to this later recalled, "In a place like Auschwitz, it was still unforeseen that someone would give up his life. It restored our faith in the human race." Father Kolbe's love did not insist on its own way, but he sacrificed everything for his brother.

Love Listens

Years ago, having just come from a hospital visit with a dying parishioner, I sat down with my family for a quiet dinner. During the meal, my third-grader excitedly told every detail of a squabble she witnessed that day on the school playground. Her story was not important to me, having just moments earlier dealt with issues of life and death. What was important was that her story was important to her. She was interested in it, and she wanted me to share her interest. I listened not so much for my sake but for her sake. My listening intently affirmed her worth. Love listens for the sake of others.

A selfish person either does not listen at all or only listens when interested in what is being said. Selfless love always seeks to be a good listener. Attentive listening is especially important during a disagreement. The person in the next-door apartment should not be the only person who listens to both sides of the argument. I recall a cute quip: "In matters controversial, my perception is quite fine. I always see both points of view ... the one that's wrong ... and mine." Love listens, gives the other person the benefit of the doubt, and does not insist on its own way.

Love Sacrifices Itself For Others

The way of Christ and his love is a well-traveled pathway of sacrifice and giving. Christ is the seeking shepherd. Christ did not come to earth to seek his own glory but our own good. His life was an example of unselfish love. In the garden of Gethsemane, the Lord could have insisted on his own way and have had the cup of agony and crucifixion taken from him. But his mission was to do the Father's will for the benefit of us all. The Christian life is to be God-centered. And when we seek to do God's will, the rest of our lives will fall into place. The greatest people our world has ever known have been those who lived their lives for others.

Awhile back, a bride and groom came to me for a premarital counseling session. "What do you love most about him?" I asked the bride-to-be. She responded: "He's always there when I need him. He lives for me. Once, while we were in college, I saw something in a store I liked and pointed it out to him. He bought it for me with the money he had set aside for his dinner. At the time, I didn't know it — but I later discovered he didn't eat that night." Love seeks not its own but gives of itself generously.

On the other hand, stopping for dinner at a restaurant some time ago, I noticed a couple on a date. The girl ordered the steak dinner. It was the most expensive item on the menu. Assessing his now diminishing financial condition, the young man ordered a hot dog. After dinner, she had the strawberry shortcake. I checked the menu and it was the top-of-the-line dessert. He had another hot dog. Perhaps she was trying to tell her date something. Selfless love was not evident as she ordered only the very best for herself.

Selfless love needs daily exercise, for our sinful, self-seeking nature can quickly destroy it. Selfless love is unnatural. If you do not believe this, let me suggest a little experiment: Put two small children on the floor with only one interesting toy between them. You will quickly see a

72

demonstration of original sin in action. Selfless love is rather supernatural in nature. It is God's love in us loving others through us. Love is a transformation from centering on me to me centering on God — who in turn helps me center on you. Where love is, God is — for God is love.

Perhaps Saint Paul provided the finest commentary on this portion of his love poem. Writing to the Philippian Christians, he said:

> *If then there is any encouragement in Christ, any consolation from love, any sharing in the Spirit, any compassion and sympathy, make my joy complete: be of the same mind, having the same love, being in full accord and of one mind. Do nothing for selfish ambition or conceit, but in humility regard others as better than yourselves. Let each of you look not to your own interests, but to the interests of others.*
> (Philippians 2:1-4)

God's love does not insist on its own way.

Reflection

1) Is there anyone in your life for whom you might be willing to give your life so that they may live?

2) When has insisting on your own way hurt you in life?

3) When have you acted like wrong way Jonah and went in the opposite direction of where God was trying to lead you?

4) God had a plan for Jonah's life; what do you feel is God's plan for your life?

5) Cite someone you know who is a good example of selfless love.

6) Tell of an occasion in which you gave of yourself unselfishly to someone other than a family member.

7) What is the difference between going to church and coming to worship?

8) How is listening to others an act of love?

9) Who in your life needs some selfless love from you?

10) When you are right, can you be wrong for insisting you are right?

SEVEN

Love Is Not Irritable Or Resentful

Christianity does not have a monopoly on ethical ideals. Classical literature provides shelves of books expounding virtuous behavior. China has its Confucius; India has its *Bhagavad Gita*; the Greeks and Romans had Plato, Aristotle, and Marcus Aurelius. All encouraged virtue. Aristotle, for example, spoke of the generosity of the "great-souled man."

But there is a great gulf between Christianity and the world's non-Christian moralists. For it is difficult to find in the pagan moralists anything quite approaching the loftiness of Saint Paul's love poem. The ancient expounders of virtue shied away from picturing humans as capable of self-surrender.

Aristotle's "great-souled man" would be ready to bear insults without striking back. For greatness of character would always strive to rise above the common person's response. Julius Caesar was a magnanimous man who frequently forgave his enemies.

His virtue did not spring from Christian love, but rather from his pride that he had the virtue of being able to forgive. The difference in Caesar's forgiveness and Christian forgiveness is a difference in motive. The "why" of our morality is the key issue. We can be outwardly virtuous for a variety of reasons. Many heathens are so-called "good people". But for Christians, having basked in the revealed love of God through Jesus Christ, we are propelled by that love to become virtuous. Ours is a morality of response not of human achievement. We seek to be obedient to God's will and to imitate God's virtue of love.

God's mighty act of love was Jesus' being hung from a cross. The Son of God, having been crucified for our benefit, must evoke from us the willingness to forgive as we have been forgiven. Through our baptism, we have become children of God. We no longer need to be yoked to touchiness or to anger or to resentment or to an unforgiving spirit. We no longer need to be irritable, for we have been yoked to Christ and can look with him at those who upset us and say, "Father, forgive them." No longer hard-hearted, we reach out to others in the spirit of God and love them. The negative, energy-sapping, debilitating emotion of bitterness and resentment can be expunged from our hearts by the indwelling of God's love.

In the Lord's Prayer we pray, "Forgive us our debts as we also have forgiven our debtors" (Matthew 6:12). In the *Large Catechism,* Martin Luther wrote, "Inasmuch as we sin greatly against God every day, and yet he forgives it through grace, we must forgive our neighbor who does us harm… If you do not forgive, do you think that God forgives you? But if you forgive, you have comfort and assurance that you are forgiven in heaven." In our forgiving, Luther rightly suggests that we can have our faith strengthened, for we know that our human nature would not of itself be able to forgive someone who hurt us greatly.

Only God in our heart can compel such forgiveness. In our act of forgiving, we know that God can and already has forgiven us.

We rejoice with Saint John who wrote, "For God so loved the world that he gave his only Son that everyone who believes in him may not perish but may have eternal life" (John 3:16). There is comfort and joy that God has loved the world in general. But we also find great joy in knowing that God's forgiving love has been focused upon us in particular. Let me suggest you now read a paraphrase of Saint John's beautiful passage and insert your name wherever there is a blank.

Here goes: "For God so loved (your name), that he gave his only Son for _____, that if _____ believes in him, _____ may not perish but _____ may have eternal life." It is a wonderful feeling to know God loves you particularly.

Isn't it curious when it comes to forgiving others, we would rather dwell in the realm of the general than in the particular? We have little problem loving the neighbor as a general concept but can have a great problem loving the neighbor next door to us. Yet, in Christ, we are called to be forgiving in particular. We are called to love and forgive even the person who is consistently arrogant and rude to us and irritates us at every turn.

Love Refuses To Be Irritated

Having been cautioned that arrogance and rudeness have no place in our Christian life, Saint Paul speaks to us of love's response to the arrogance and rudeness of others. Yes, it is difficult for us not to become irritated when we are called upon to endure the cavalier treatment of others. Yet, love refuses to be irritated by the display of ingratitude which people sometimes return for kindness shown to them. Love that has drunk so freely from God's artesian well of forgiveness is not touchy. It is not quick to take offense.

Becoming quickly irritated could well be an outward demonstration of an inward condition of pride and self-love. We become angry when our vanity is hurt. Earlier we saw that the disciples of our Lord quarreled among themselves over the place of honor when the Lord entered his kingdom. They were particularly angered by the sons of Zebedee whose mother pleaded on their behalf. Maybe they were disappointed that their own mothers hadn't gotten to Jesus first. Their pride was hurt, so they were irritated. But the more excellent way of love commends a more generous forgiving reaction.

Petty annoyances are a major part of everyday life. We need to go with the flow of both the bad and the good in life. Some time ago, I stopped at a rather long red light at a major intersection. After waiting more than a minute, I was startled by an angry blast of foul language coming from the car next to me. Sheepishly turning to investigate, I expected to see two passengers in fisticuffs. Tuning into the tirade, I discovered, somewhat to my relief, that the red light was the object of the driver's rage.

The light was not broken and stuck on red; it was just quietly doing its job. But at this particular moment, there was no oncoming traffic, and it was quite possible to proceed across the intersection safely. The red light prevented this, and the driver was beside himself. The day was beautiful, but the driver allowed his irritable nature to become infuriated by a red light. He made his life miserable over nothing.

On another equally gorgeous day, I was driving with a local funeral director to the cemetery. How easy it would have been for him to be irritated and complain on having to work on such a fine day. Instead, he commented to me on how much he was enjoying the ride. Picking up on his comment, I said, "You really have it made. You get to take a wonderful drive on a beautiful day — in a Cadillac no less — and you are getting paid, to boot." A beautiful day has a charm of its own — no matter whether we are stuck at a long red light or are on our way to a cemetery.

Every minute we allow ourselves to be irritated, we forfeit sixty seconds of happiness.

When we allow irritability to invade our lives, other unsavory spirits sometimes follow. From irritation, anger can quickly spring. Speaking while we are angry, we often make speeches we later regret. A friend of mine says that you can't unscramble an egg. Once your angry words are out, there is no way to retrieve them. Then there are those who simply shirk off their anger and try to excuse their bad temper by saying it is over within a moment. If you are one of these folks, remember the same is true of a shotgun that takes a mere moment to blow everything to pieces. Those with a sharp tongue must be aware that they are apt to cut their own throats. Allowing ourselves to become irritated is both ungodly and unwise. Christian love is not irritable.

Those who are self-centered are often easily annoyed. Some have not moved far from the infantile stage of believing that they are the center of the universe. And if they have, some see themselves through the eyes of their mother and have an inflated sense of themselves. Even if we are blessed with good looks, wealth, and brains, all are gifts from God. Therefore all praise and honor should be lavished on God.

Back in the fourteenth century, a monk announced to the people of his village that on the coming Sunday he would preach the greatest sermon he had ever preached on God's love. He begged everyone to be present. At the appropriate hour, the cathedral was filled with young and old. They went through the usual communion liturgy. The monk held his sermon to the very end of the service. When it was finally time for the sermon, everyone was anxiously anticipating the promised discourse of the monk. Instead of ascending into the pulpit as he usually did, the monk went to a candelabrum and removed a long burning candle. He then walked to the altar where a wooden figure of Christ was nailed to a cross. He silently lifted the candle until the glow was right underneath one of the pierced hands of Jesus. He held it there with his back to the congregation. He held it for several minutes before he shifted and held the candle below the other pierced hand of the Lord. After another long period, he held it along Christ's side where the spear had pierced him. Then he dropped to his knees in prayer holding the candle so the candle lighted the pierced feet of Jesus.

After praying for a long time, he stood, turned around, and faced the congregation. The candle now lighted his face, and the people could see the gentle and affectionate tears flowing down his cheeks. He finally spoke his first words, "My beloved people, this is my sermon on the love of God for you." Then he dismissed them with the benediction.

Love Is Not Resentful

Jesus could have been so irritated and resentful when he was crucified. Instead he is tender, kind, and forgiving. Paul's plea is that we allow the spirit of Christ to dwell in us. Jesus, who was reviled, reviled not in return. He met the envy, bitterness, and hatred that impaled him on the tree of death with a cleansing torrent of love. As Saint Peter said, "Do not repay evil for evil or abuse for abuse, but, on the contrary, repay with a blessing" (1 Peter 3:9). Love is not quick to take offense but is longsuffering.

In the long run, we'll even be happier when we give people a bit of our love rather than a piece of our mind. Instead of being so anxious to put someone in their place, we might try putting ourselves in their place. Prior to possessing a deeper understanding of all that love entails, we may well have been as irascible as them. People do not need to taste our wrath but rather a sample of the unconditional love of God through us.

A Christian soldier in a Scottish regiment was asked how he was brought to Christ. He related the following:

> There was a private in our company who was converted at Malta before the regiment came to Egypt. We sure gave that fellow an awful time. The devil got possession of me, and I made that man's life miserable. Well, one night...a terrible, wet night... he came in from sentry watch. He was very tired and wet, and before getting into bed, he got down on his knees to

pray. My boots were heavy, for they were caked with mud. I threw one, and it hit him on the side of his head, and the other one bounced off of his back. But he just went on with his prayers. The next morning I found my boots beautifully cleaned and polished by the side of my bed. This was his reply to me.

It just broke my heart, and that morning I was saved. I gave my life to Christ. Love had won me over.

Love is not resentful; it does not keep a record of wrongs. Those of us who are prone to resentment keep a careful accounting of all slights, both real and imagined. These wounds to our self-esteem collect and simmer and periodically boil over into angry words and nasty deeds. The greater the number of entries, the more difficult it becomes to later erase them. Molehills easily and quickly grow into mountains. Love makes good use of the eraser end of the pencil to cleanse the record. Perhaps even more importantly, it does not use the graphite end of the pencil to add to it.

There Is No Anger With Love

An ancient proverb goes, "Whom the gods would destroy, they first make angry." A young lion and a mountain goat went to the same watering hole to quench their thirst. One day, when they arrived exactly at the same time, they fell into a heated argument as to who would drink first. Soon, they became so enraged that both were determined to fight each other to the death. Ceasing their battle for a moment to catch their breath, they looked up and noticed a flock of vultures hovering overhead waiting for the loser to fall. The quarrel quickly ended.

Even when our anger doesn't lock us in mortal combat, it is not good for our health. The person was right who said, "Every time I get angry, I drive a nail in my coffin." Anger destroys. In anger, Cain killed his brother; Moses cast down the tablets of the law; the elder son refused to go to the prodigal son's coming home party; Peter cut off the ear of the priest's slave. Anger often turns destructive.

Anger can be controlled. Consider the executive who controls his anger all day at work, then acts very childlike and has a temper tantrum at home. A person in the middle of blowing their top at home can, in the next instant, handle an important telephone call from the boss in perfect calm. We can turn anger on, and we can turn it off. If we control just one moment of anger, we will likely escape many days of sorrow.

Resentment also has a way of enslaving. We become a slave of the one we resent. Thinking about this person, happiness drains out of us. The resented person goes with us wherever we go. If we are consumed with resentment for this person, we can go out to the finest restaurant and have the best of everything, and yet we might as well have eaten at a fast food dive. We eat the gourmet meal, but the person we resent consumes our thoughts and keeps us from enjoying it.

Love Is Forgetful

Some people say, "I can forgive but I can't forget." Saint Paul would say that such an attitude was unchristian. For him, it was impossible to completely forgive someone without also forgetting their offense. Our Lord is most forgetful of our sins once they are forgiven. God's love, when it also dwells in us, not only forgives another but forgets their offense. When we neither forgive nor forget, our lives are enslaved by bitterness and resentment.

We are able to select what we remember. Therefore, we can deliberately forget the arrogance and unkindness that is often directed our way. We who are very good at forgetting our own faults need to be just as competent in forgetting the slights of others. To blot these things out of our minds is god-like. Perhaps we should raise Christian forgetfulness to the rank of virtue. It is good for us to forgive. It is even better to forget.

Snow is hardly news in many parts of our nation. After a blizzard, it takes a snowplow to tackle the snowdrifts and help us become mobile again. If resentments are like snow-drifts, then forgiveness would be the snowplow. Forgiveness opens roads again as it removes barriers, and forgetfulness prevents future blockages. It is said that Abraham Lincoln never forgot a kindness nor remembered a wrong. This is a worthy goal for all of us to aspire to, for love is not irritable or resentful.

Reflection

1) How does Christian love and forgiveness differ from other religions and moralists?

2) Do you feel God's particular love and forgiveness?

3) Who does God want you to love and forgive in particular?

4) What especially annoys and irritates you, and what might you do to curb its negative effect on your life?

5) What did you think of the monk's sermon, and how might it have affected you?

6) What are some negative things that people have done to you that you might still need to forgive?

7) How can resentment be a form of enslavement in your life?

8) How has anger and resentment lessened your life?

9) Tell of a time someone has generously forgiven you and what it did for you.

10) When we forgive someone, why is it just as important to also forget their offense?

EIGHT

Love Does Not Rejoice In Wrongdoing But Rejoices In The Truth

Love is not only forgetful of wrongs committed against it, but it also turns a deaf ear to unsavory stories it hears about others. Love takes no pleasure in learning about the failures of others or the wickedness they commit. There is no gloating over people's mistakes.

"Did you hear? Bill was riding a bike and fell off and broke his leg."

"You've got to be kidding, he is too old to be riding a bicycle; he should have had better sense."

Here we have a little dialogue between two friends who both know poor, old Bill. My guess is that at least one of the two was smiling widely during their dialogue. Why do we smile, even laugh, sometimes when we hear about the misfortune of others? Laughter may be a relief mechanism within us that produces a joyous response that the misfortune happened to Bill rather than to us. We are not rejoicing overtly at Bill's misfortune, but perhaps there is a bit of joy that the fates did in Bill rather than us. Few of us have enough love in our hearts to rather say, "Poor Bill, I wish I would have broken my leg instead of him."

Perhaps even worse, how do we respond to a juicy piece of gossip about someone we detest? It could be the person who beat us out of a promotion. Or, it could be gossip about the one who got a date with the special person we really liked. Maybe it concerns the person who goes out of her way to make our lives miserable. When we hear that one of these people really messed up, it is hard not to gloat. "I know he is no good," we say, feeling completely justified in our negative feelings about the person. Saint Paul tells us that love is never glad when others do wrong. The malicious delight we sometimes feel when we hear about the misfortunes of others is not Christlike at all.

Another aspect of this naturally sinful tendency is that we think we look better as a result of another person's shortcomings. A clergy serving a church that is losing members looks at a neighboring church that is losing people twice as fast and feels good that the neighboring church is worse off than his. Then in conversation with church council members, the pastor frequently brings up the faltering neighboring church and maybe piously says, "Isn't it too bad that Trinity lost a hundred members last year? We lost fifty." Now, if Trinity gained one hundred more people than it lost, few pastors would make this wonderful news part of a report to their parish leadership. How much better that the pastor acknowledges the parish that is growing and learns from it. Having learned the reasons for their success, the pastor should apply what she learns to benefit the parish she is serving.

Making ourselves appear superior by comparison to someone inferior does not emanate out of Christian love. To seek to make ourselves look good at the expense of others is, of itself, an exercise in not looking good.

Love Turns A Deaf Ear To Gossip

Love takes no delight in listening to scandal, however authentic the account may be. We are not to rejoice in evil. Evil is hurtful to people; Christ came to save us from evil. Therefore, rejoicing in evil is an activity in opposition to Christ. The issue is not whether the gossip is true or false, but whether it is edifying. If it is not helpful, then we need to keep it to ourselves. John Wesley, one of the founders of the

Methodist church, said that a person who loves enjoys those things that bring glory to God and promotes goodwill among people. Malicious gossip is not edifying to either our God or our neighbor.

There are three tests any bit of gossip needs to pass before it is shared from one Christian to another. First, is it true… true beyond any shadow of doubt? Is it certifiably true? Some time ago, three couples from a parish I served went away for a weekend together. One morning they all met together in one of their motel rooms to plan the day. It happened that two of the people left the meeting together to get something from their respective rooms. It was a man and a woman who were not married to one another.

As they left the motel room together, two other parishioners who just happened to be in the same motel saw them exiting the motel room together. Not knowing the situation, they thought the obvious and quickly turned away, embarrassed at what they saw. The two coming out of the room together called to them and prevented a terrible misunderstanding from happening. Even that which we observe with our own two eyes may not be as it appears.

The second test needs to answer the question of whether sharing something is kind and helpful to the people involved. Even if the two people exiting the motel room were having an affair and we caught them, it would still not be kind or helpful to gossip about what we saw.

Third, does telling this story in some way strengthen the body of Christ and give glory to God? If two members of the church were having an affair, I do not see how sharing this with others would strengthen the body of Christ and give glory to God.

If all three of these questions can be answered in the affirmative, then please share the information with others. For if what we observe or hear from someone else is true without a doubt, if it is kind and helpful to those involved, if it is edifying to the church and gives glory to God, then we must by all means share it.

Many feel that the most powerful part of a person's anatomy is that little, movable, muscular structure attached to the floor of the mouth. All of us have at one time been victimized by another person's tongue. In Shakespeare's play *Othello,* Iago stands in awe of the tongue's power when he says, "Who steals my purse steals trash, but he who filches from me my good name makes me poor indeed." God commands that we say nothing about our neighbor which would even slightly tarnish his name. God wishes that we defend our neighbor, speak well of him and put the best construction on everything.

"Watch your mouth!" How often have we said this to children who were giving us a bad time? Perhaps our parents said it to us. In one sense, Saint Paul is saying that to us, for tongue power is awesome power. All of us would do well to pray the prayer of the psalmist: "Set a guard over my mouth, O Lord; keep watch over the door of my lips" (Psalm 141:3). Instead of rejoicing at wrong, love rejoices in the right. It is always eager to believe the best. Love searches out the goodness in a person and is always happy to discover it. This magnanimous spirit is one of the marks of a life filled with the spirit of Christ.

Love Seeks Out The Good In Others

As I mentioned in an earlier chapter, I ask couples that I am marrying, "What do you really love about him/her? What are his/her best qualities?" After they answer my two questions, I tell them that most couples do not sit around thinking about what is good about their spouse and what they do right. Rather, they center upon what they do not like about one another. "It is important," I continue, "that you affirm one another in your marriage and often tell each other what you love about the other." Saint Paul calls upon us to give thanks to God and to rejoice in the good qualities of our spouse as well as the rest of our family and with everyone with whom we are associated.

Our Lord always had an eye out for the good qualities in others. He rejoiced over the commendable acts of centurions, fishermen, Samaritans, and even prostitutes. As we dwell on what is good in someone, the darker side of their personality will also become less apparent to us.

All people long for others to appreciate their good qualities. Appreciation also brings out the best in people. Psychologists tell us that praise produces desirable behavior more readily than punishment. The story is told of a Scottish minister that upon his death, someone said of him, "There is no one left in our village now to appreciate the triumphs of ordinary folks." A spirit that celebrates people's good qualities produces an even larger harvest of these attributes.

Perhaps it is a bit simplistic, but most people can be put into one of two categories; either they are positive people or negative people. The negative people are always looking for something to criticize. Dwelling upon someone's weakness, they rejoice when that person screws up. They are the gossips, the backbiters, those who blame themselves only after exhausting all other possibilities. Their spouse can have nine strengths, and they will dwell on their one weakness. Love seeks out the positive — not the negative.

Positive people are exemplified in a wonderful true story. A Johns Hopkins professor gave a group of graduate students an assignment to go to the slums of Baltimore and investigate the backgrounds and environments of 200 boys between the ages of 12 and 16. Afterwards, they were to predict the boys' chances for a wholesome future. The students consulted social statistics, talked to the boys, and compiled as much data as they could. They then predicted that a very high percentage of the boys would spend some time in jail.

Twenty-five years later, another group of graduate students was given the job of testing the prediction. They returned to the same slum area. Some of the boys, now men, were still living there. Others had died and some had moved away. Surprisingly, they were able to get in touch with 180 of the original 200. They found that only four of the group had ever been sent to jail. Why was it that these men, who had lived in a place rampant with crime, had such a good record? The researchers were continually told by those they interviewed, "Well, there was this teacher...." They pressed further and found that in 75% of the cases it was the same woman. The researchers found the teacher who was now living in a retirement home.

They wanted to know how she exerted this remarkably positive influence over this group of slum children. Could she give them any reason why so many of these boys remembered her? "What did you do to these boys? Can you tell us?" they pressed her. "No," she said, "I can't remember anything specific." Then, thinking back over the years, she said musingly, more to herself than to her questioners, "I loved those boys." She loved them, treated them with positive expectations, and most of them grew up as responsible people. Love that is eager to believe the best in others most often finds it and nourishes it.

In the Bible, in Saint Paul's letter to the Philippian Christians, he wrote, "Finally, beloved, whatever is true, whatever is honorable, whatever is just, whatever is pure, whatever is pleasing, whatever is commendable, if there is any excellence, if there is anything worthy of praise, think about these things" (Philippians 4:8).

Love is always eager to rejoice in the truth and to believe the best about someone.

Reflection

1) Share an instance when someone shared something negative about you that was both wrong and hurtful.

2) Why is it when we hear something negative about someone, we often find it pleasing to share it with others?

3) Tell of a time when you discovered you were completely wrong about a person or an event you initially felt negative about.

4) Why is hurtful gossip wrong, even when the information you are sharing is true?

5) Why is trying to look good at the expense of others in itself an exercise of not looking good?

6) What are the three tests any bit of gossip needs to pass before it can be shared?

7) Why is your tongue the most powerful part of your body for good and for evil?

8) Share something good about another person that you are happy about.

9) What about you is worthy of praise?

10) Love at least three people this week by telling each of them what you especially like about them.

NINE

Love Bears All Things

The magnificent climax of Saint Paul's exalted speech on love begins with the statement that love "bears all things, believes all things, hopes all things, endures all things" (1 Corinthians 13:7). So comprehensive and powerful is Christian love that nothing can escape its broad reach. No person or situation is off limits to powerful love. It is the same Paul who writes, "I can do all things through him who strengthens me" (Philippians 4:13). All things become possible with perfect love dwelling in our hearts.

During the course of the Civil War, when news reached Washington that General Lee was about to surrender, Lincoln left at once for Richmond. Brushing aside the suggestion that there should be a triumphal procession, the president walked through the streets of Richmond alone. Heartsick and weary, with head bowed, he went into Jefferson Davis' home. Entering the office of the rebel president, he sat down with his head in his hands. His giant frame began to shake with sobs. Lincoln — blood brother of the men who wore the gray, a leader of the men who wore the blue — was weeping for all the boys of the North and South who would never again return home to their families. In his great heart, he carried the burdens of his nation's anguish.

One could readily understand Lincoln feeling the burden of loss for the families of the blue, but because of his great love, he equally felt the burden of loss for those who wore the gray. Their offense which threatened the union was covered by tears of compassion that sprang from a loving and forgiving heart. His enemy's burden was also Lincoln's burden.

A love that bears all things is one that not only endures when negative things comes its way, but more than that, it is a quality of love that also bears the burdens of another person's failings. As Christ bore the penalty for our sins, we sometimes bear the consequences of another person's mistakes and bear them with a forgiving and loving heart. Recognizing that there is no one free from weakness, no one without a load to carry, no one all sufficient, and no one who can completely go it alone, it is our Christian calling to support one another and bear one another's burdens. Love has no limit to its endurance. There is nothing love finds itself unwilling to face.

Love Bears The Cross For Others

Love shows restraint and forbearance when confronted with wrong. It sometimes is even called upon to quickly bear the blame when it is not at fault. We, who have benefited from Christ's sacrificial love, are sometimes called to bear quietly the cross placed upon us by others. Christ's followers must manifest the mind and spirit of their Lord. Vicarious suffering is one of the highest expressions of love when it bears the burden of another's failure.

Sometimes we are even called upon to bear the burden of giving up a sacred principle. We are called upon to exhibit the higher calling of love. Having been an army chaplain, I recall the story of three chaplains during World War II who made friends with a German baron in a prisoner of war camp. They promised to visit him at his castle after the war.

Keeping their promise, they discovered that the castle was almost completely bombed out. Their baron friend was living in one small room amid all the wreckage. He was thrilled that they kept their promise. From under his bed he quickly produced a bottle of vintage champagne which he proudly offered his guests in celebration of their visit. One chaplain said, "I'm sorry, but I am a minister and I do not drink." The second begged off for the same reason. The third chaplain saw the hurt look on the baron's face, having already uncorked the fine champagne to honor his guests. He said, "I don't drink either, but minister or not, one of us has to be a Christian." He then drank a toast with the baron. There are times when even our most precious principles must give way to the higher law of love.

Mahatma Gandhi's nonviolent approach to achieving change was consistent with the teachings of Christ. Jesus taught, "But I say to you, love your enemies and pray for those who persecute you" (Matthew 5:44). Then again, "But I say to you, do not resist an evil doer. But if anyone strikes you on the right cheek, turn the other also" (Matthew 5:39). Inspired by Gandhi, Dr. Martin Luther King Jr. became a powerful example of a love which bears all things. As he became more deeply committed to the civil rights movement, Dr. King's life was in constant danger. There were marches, sit-ins, and strikes. A bomb exploded on the front porch of his home...luckily his wife and children were in the rear of the house and were not hurt. There were numerous threats on his life; he was stabbed in Harlem, jailed several times, and pelted with rocks. To all of this, Reverend King responded by telling his followers that they should not turn to violence under any circumstance. He saw himself and the movement he led as following not only the teachings of Gandhi but more importantly the way of Jesus Christ and the way of the cross.

In April 1968, Dr. King was invited to Memphis, Tennessee to start another march. This time it would be in support of striking sanitation workers. His plane from Atlanta was searched for bombs. In his speech there on April 3, Reverend King spoke prophetically, "But it really doesn't matter with me now, because I have been to the mountaintop. And I've looked over, and I've seen the promised land. I may not get there with you. But I want you to know tonight that we as a people will get to the promised land. So I'm happy tonight. I'm not worried about anything. I'm not fearing any man. Mine eyes have seen the glory of the coming of the Lord." It was his last speech. The next day Dr. King met with his helpers in his motel room. A bit later, while on the balcony outside his room, an assassin's lethal bullet found its mark, and Martin Luther King Jr. died an hour later.

On Tuesday, April 9, the funeral began. Inside the Ebenezer Baptist Church in Atlanta were many famous people. Outside were thousands of ordinary folks. Many words were spoken, but the words which touched people the most were spoken by Reverend King himself. A tape recording of part of his last sermon in his church was played. His voice said,

If any of you are around when I have to meet my day, I don't want a long funeral. And if you get somebody to deliver the eulogy, tell him not to talk too long. Tell him not to mention that I have a Nobel Peace Prize. That isn't important. Tell him not to mention that I have three hundred or four hundred other awards. That's not important. I'd like someone to mention that day that Martin Luther King Jr. tried to give his life serving others. I'd like for someone to say that day that Martin Luther King, Jr. tried to love somebody. I want you to be able to say that day that I did try to feed the hungry. I want you to be able to say that I did try in my life to clothe the naked. I want you to be able to say on that day that I did try in my life to visit those who were in prison. And I want you to say that I tried to love and serve humanity.

Love Keeps On Giving

Love does not condone wrong. Wrong must often be exposed and condemned. But a life filled with love seeking a better and more just world is non-violent in its nature and its application. It is a long-suffering love, one that keeps on giving, one that excludes no one...not even an enemy. This kind of love receives its strength and direction from Christ himself.

Love's willingness to bear all things inspired the great figures of history like Abraham Lincoln and Martin Luther King, Jr. The Christian martyrs of every period of history loved Christ so much that they died for their faith. Their legacy still moves us today. We are especially touched and inspired as we consider Christ being crucified on Calvary's cross. We are also called upon to consider what we ourselves need to bear lovingly. In some cases, it is an abusive spouse or one afflicted with alcoholism. It could be a child or other family member who has greatly disappointed us. Perhaps we are sick or even terminally ill. Can we even bear this with grace and use it to God's glory?

My mentor, Reverend Edward H. Stammel, was diagnosed with terminal cancer. He was told that he had only three months to live. At the time he had been invited back to his former church (where he served for over thirty years) to preach at an anniversary service. His cancer went into remission allowing him to return and preach.

On the special day, he ascended the familiar pulpit to deliver his much-anticipated sermon. He began, "I want to begin by thanking all of you, for you prayed me here." While leaning over the side of the pulpit with his arm outstretched and his finger pressing an imaginary button, he continued, "I was standing in the vestibule of heaven, and God reached out and put his finger on the hold button."

He lived several more months and used his imminent death to even more poignantly proclaim his love for the Lord. Instead of basking in self-pity, he boldly witnessed that he would soon join his Lord in paradise. Love's virtue glows even more brightly as it seeks to bear all things... even our own death.

Reflection

1) What can you learn from Lincoln's reaction to the losses of both his friends and his enemies?

2) What did Martin Luther King Jr. feel was worth remembering about his life?

3) For what might you wish to be remembered?

4) Can you recall someone whose great faith and ability to deal with adversity inspired you?

5) What is one of the most difficult things you have had to bear in your life?

6) Give an example when you lovingly bore the burden of another person's failure?

7) Give an example when love compelled you to go against one of your principles.

8) Who in your life is God calling you to especially love by bearing with them?

9) Tell of someone you knew who died gracefully.

10) If you were told you had just three months to live, what would be something that you would want to be sure to do?

TEN

Love Believes All Things

A loving spirit is always prone to believe the best about others. Its attitude is to put the best construction upon their motives, even at times when their actions seem to indicate otherwise. It walks the second and often the third mile trusting and believing in the person before it reluctantly is forced to see the negative side of their actions. Love looks for and most often finds the best in the other person.

John Kasten was my 85-year-old friend. When it came to me, he found little-to-nothing to criticize. He was blind to my faults and saw only my good points. "Pastor, I think you are the greatest, and I'll always stick by you," John told me many times. When others would complain to John about me, he would hear nothing of it. When I buried my friend John, I buried one of God's special blessings to me.

There are always a lot of people who can clearly see our faults. There are fewer who have a balanced view of both our strengths and our weaknesses. Other than perhaps our mother, we are lucky to have one or two people in our lives who search out our best qualities, are blind to our faults, and believe the best about us. Surely their assessment is somewhat unrealistic, but it is no less pleasant. John Kasten was that kind of person for me. I miss him.

Even when someone is not at his or her best, love sees more than even an honest eye can see. It sees the person beneath the facts. And even when everything comes up negative, it looks through the eyes of God and still loves the person. For we are reminded yet again that God's love was so great for all of us that God did not spare even his Son on our behalf. Love believes the person is of inestimable worth, is redeemable, and can change for the good.

Years ago, I saw the classic play *Man of La Mancha*. I believe it illustrates well what I am saying. The Man of La Mancha came to a wayside inn. He was an ordinary man out of touch with reality, and he believed he was a knight. He saw Aldonza, the waitress there. She was also the local prostitute. Aldonza was dirty and smelled from perspiration. "Ho, my lady. You will be my lady... every knight needs a lady, and you will be my lady. And I will give you a new name. It will no longer be Aldonza but Dulcinea." She looked at him in amazement. "Me your lady? Ha!" She kicked up her heels, grabbed a sack of money out of his hand, and ran off the stage. Every time the Man of La Mancha saw her, he said, "You are a lady; you have a new name; I have given it to you; it is Dulcinea."

The curtain went up on another scene, and the stage is empty. It was nighttime. Suddenly, Aldonza came on stage. Her hair was disheveled; she had blood and mud on her; her skirt was torn. She had been raped. Hysterical, she ran confused and crying to the middle of the stage. Off to the side entered the Man of La Mancha. When he saw her, he said, "Ho, my lady." To which she replied, "Don't call me a lady. Look at me, I was born in a ditch; my mother left me naked and cold and too hungry to cry. I never blamed her; I'm sure she left hoping I would have the good sense to die. Ah... look at me, I'm no lady; I'm only a kitchen slut, reeking with sweat, a strumpet men use and forget. Oh God, I am no lady; I am only Aldonza. I am nothing at all." She ran away and was gone.

In the last scene, the Man of La Mancha, like Jesus of Nazareth, had been despised, rejected by men, a man of sorrow, and acquainted with grief. He was dying from a broken heart. While on his deathbed, a courtly woman walked over to his side. She had a beautiful mantilla that covered her modestly. She knelt beside his deathbed and said, "My lord, my lord." Through a haze, he looks at her and asks, "Who are you?"

"My lord, look – don't you remember? Try to remember, my lord. You sang the song, remember… to dream the impossible dream, to fight the unbeatable foe? My lord, you gave me a new name. You called me your lady." And through eyes clouded with death he recognized her and said, "Dulcinea!" and he died.

Christ's great love for humankind enabled him to find good in all kinds of common and even unsavory characters. He believed the best about them – which, in turn, inspired many of them to do their best. People often live up to our expectations, both good and bad. Believe the worst about people, and they are not likely to disappoint you.

Love that believes all things sees no limit to the power of God. It believes God can do all things. On an African safari, I once had two, fully grown, male lions walk past our safari vehicle. I could almost reach out and touch them. I had forgotten how big and powerful a lion was until I was that close to one. They are majestic and intimidating creatures. Had I not been safe in a large vehicle… well, that would have been a sorry story.

Daniel's Belief In God Was Miraculously Rewarded

In the Old Testament, Daniel's experience with lions was not as pleasant. Nothing separated Daniel from the lions as he was dumped into a place filled with the hungry beasts. There have been many terrible ways people have been killed which are recorded in human history, but being dumped into a den filled with lions and having a stone placed over the opening leaving you in total darkness, must rank among the worst.

On the surface, it would appear that Daniel must have done something terrible to merit such treatment. His crime was that he continued to pray to the God of the Hebrews three times a day ignoring a new law that no one should make a petition to anyone except King Darius for a period of thirty days.

For years, Daniel had been in exile; and although he had distinguished himself as a brilliant and capable leader... one who could even interpret the future... the law of the Medes and Persians could not be revoked.

Some leaders, jealous of Daniel, had set a trap for him. It was too late when King Darius saw through it. All day, Darius tried to find a way out for Daniel, but he was unsuccessful. He had to follow the new law he had been tricked into making by Daniel's enemies. "May your God, whom you faithfully serve, deliver you!" (Daniel 6:16), Darius said to Daniel as he was placed into the dangerous den of death and was greeted by hungry lions.

All night, Darius neither ate nor slept. At daybreak he ran to the den of lions. As he came near the den he cried out in an anguished tone, "O Daniel, servant of the living God, has your God whom you faithfully serve been able to deliver you from the lions?" (Daniel 6:20). Joy filled Darius' heart as he heard the voice of Daniel saying, "My God sent his angel and shut the lions' mouths so that they would not hurt me" (Daniel 6:22).

Before being cast into the lions' den, it appeared that Daniel would have fared better had he taken a vacation from worshiping God for thirty days. He, too, knew that his jealous enemies had set a trap for him. Instead of taking the easy way out, Daniel saw in the crisis facing him an opportunity to witness to his faith and trust in Almighty God whom he loved and worshiped. He would not accommodate himself to a safer solution.

Daniel believed that his task was to live nobly and faithfully each day and to leave the problems he might face tomorrow in the hands of his just and righteous God. The evil in the world that would cast him into a den of lions was not his God's doing. Evil is powerful; it can be frightening and painful and often deadly. But loyalty to almighty God was more important than anything else, and even death was to be welcomed over unfaithfulness.

One can almost see the smirks on the faces of Daniel's enemies as he is being fed to the lions. From all appearances, Daniel's God had deserted him. Initially, there were no signs of God's intervention; no army of angels marching to Daniel's rescue, nor bolts of lightning consuming his accusers. As the stone was placed over the opening of the den and sealed, Daniel's God was nowhere to be seen. "Was he hiding?" "Was he asleep?" They may have taunted. Yet, we know where Daniel's God was; God was in the den right there with Daniel directing the angels to hold shut the salivating mouths of the lions. God was there protecting Daniel and sustaining him in his time of anguish. The God who also protected Shadrach, Meshach, and Abednego from the lapping flames of the fiery furnace now held at bay the lions as they longingly licked their chops, hoping for a quick meal.

With God's Help, All Things Are Possible

We must never forget that God does not put us in harm's way. Likewise, God does not leave us when life lays us low. Even the heroes of faith had their share of hard times. Trusting in the Lord is not a free ticket to Disney World. The lions of the world are not all caged at the local zoo. Saint Peter says in the New Testament that the devil, like a lion, prowls around seeking someone to devour. As people of faith, we cannot always avoid walking through the valleys of despair and death, but we believe that God walks in those valleys alongside of us. Believing all things, we know that with God's help, all things are possible.

The Good Shepherd walks with us and comforts us. Walking with God, we realize that neither height, nor depth, nor fiery furnaces, nor dangerous lions' dens, nor cancer, nor other tragedies life flings at us, can separate us from the love of God in Christ Jesus.

There is a wonderful little story about a little boy having difficulty lifting a heavy object. His father saw his son struggling and asked the boy whether he was using all of his strength. A bit irritated by his dad's question, he told his father that he really was. "No, you are not," replied his father, "you have not asked me for my help." As we struggle alone with the burden of life's problems, perhaps God is saying this to us as well.

Many executives have two receptacles on their desks... one for incoming mail and other papers and one for outgoing mail and work. I once read about a Christian executive who had a third receptacle. It was labeled, "With God, All Things Are Possible." Each of us has things in our lives that need to be placed in such a receptacle. We should *not* use it sparingly.

Some people believe that being a "good Christian" is a downer. They think that you need to make two lists... one list of all of the things you like to do and the other of those things that you do not like to do. Then you must abandon most of the things you like to do and do those things that you do not like to do.

This is not the way it is at all. Suppose my child, when she was younger, came to me and said, "Daddy, I love you, and I'll do anything you want me to do." Can you imagine me saying, "Andrea, this is just the moment I have been waiting for; you must get rid of all of your toys, have no friends, lock yourself in your room and become the unhappiest child in the world"? If she were to exhibit such a loving trust in me, her father, I would break my back even more to do everything in my power to enhance her life and make her happy.

Our heavenly Father does likewise. When we believe in God with all our heart, with all of our mind, and with all of our soul, we give our God the opportunity to love us even more and to further enhance our lives. Jesus said, "I came that they might have life and have it abundantly" (John 10:10). I will take him at his word and gladly seek to do his will.

Love does not throw in the towel, whether it is facing difficult situations in our own lives or in the lives of others. We do not lose faith either in ourselves or in others. One indispensable quality needed to achieve the best outcome is to believe that with God's help, the best is possible. When love believes all things, it also receives many of the most important and joyous things life has to offer. Loving and believing in God, ourselves, and others is part of love's greatness.

Reflection

1) Tell of someone in your life who believed in you and who saw you as someone even better than who you are. How did that make you feel?

2) In the play, *Man of La Mancha,* how was Aldonza transformed into Dulcinea?

3) Who in your life do you need to believe in more and see through the forgiving and loving eyes of God?

4) What lesson did you receive from the story of Daniel in the lions' den?

5) How has your faith been put to the test like Daniel's?

6) Tell of a time when you felt that you were being fed to the lions and God intervened.

7) Like the example of the executive, what do you need to put in a receptacle labeled, "With God All Things Are Possible?"

8) Why are our lives enhanced when we entrust them more completely to God?

9) What keeps you from trusting in others? How can God help you?

10) Since love believes all things, what about yourself do you need to believe in more?

ELEVEN

Love Hopes All Things

"It's hopeless." Few phrases in the English language are sadder sounding than this one. Above the entrance of Dante's hell is the inscription, "Abandon all hope, ye who enter here." On the other hand, God is the source of hope and its sustaining power.

Perhaps upon the gates of heaven there will be another sign, "This is the place of hope fulfilled; leave all despair behind."

Forty years ago, our local Lutheran High School had a financial crisis that seemed hopeless. Above and beyond a million dollar mortgage, it had acquired a million dollars of other debts due to poor management. About four months into the school year, the school ran out of money. Its financial picture was so poor that the banks would not loan the school any more money. There was no more money to pay their teachers or anything else. It was at the point of hopeless bankruptcy.

As the pastor of the church that founded the high school, I mounted a crisis fundraising campaign based upon prayer and a strong faith that God both desired and was able to save this vital ministry.

The theme of our effort was, "With God's Help, All Things Are Possible." At no time in the previous 25-year history of the school did it raise anywhere close to the money needed now to save it. In the first few months of our effort, enough money was raised to keep the school open, to pay the staff, and to pay the mortgage and other expenses. Over $800,000 was eventually donated; the school was saved, and it continues until today to provide an excellent Christian education to over 600 children. My involvement in the effort to save the Lutheran high school was only one day a week. God's involvement was clearly full time. God is the source of hope – even in hopeless situations.

I believe there are few hopeless situations; there are only hopeless attitudes. Today's church is in crisis. Eighty percent of Christian churches are barely holding their own or are declining. Some experts predict that in the next ten years, one third of all churches will close. When their church is caught in a downward spiral, many see it as a hopeless situation. I see it as a time to become more faithful and to invoke God's direction and power in turning things around. I have experienced God's miracles multiple times during my ministry and have witnessed declining churches become vibrant again.

In my recent book, *From Surviving to Thriving – A Practical Guide to Revitalize Your Church,* I have written on just this. In this book, I not only share things I have learned in fifty years of ministry that are helpful to revitalize struggling churches, but as importantly, I write about what God has done in many situations to transform what others deemed as hopeless.

Love Doesn't Throw In The Towel

A love that hopes all things goes on hoping for the best – even if there is no easily discernable ground for such hope. This is one of the distinctive characteristics of the Christian life. It was one of the attributes of our Lord. He saw possibilities in a bunch of ordinary fishermen from Galilee, in despised tax collectors, in a Roman centurion, and in a woman of questionable character named Mary Magdalene.

He did not even lose hope in a former bitter enemy of the young Christian church...none other than the esteemed author of our love poem, Saint Paul himself. Jesus came to Saul (later known as Paul) as he was on his way to persecute Christians in Damascus. There, Jesus turned his life around.

The people in the Corinthian church to which Saint Paul wrote could be particularly trying and hard to love. Many were also hopelessly unlikable. They were often bitter and argumentative. They had a chip on their shoulder and would much rather find fault than dwell on something that was laudable.

Since biblical times, the church has had this kind of person in its ranks. These are the people who are forever unhappy. They only seem to be happy when they are unhappy. They are the ones who are undermining everything. Distrustful of the pastor, upset with the church council, they are purveyors of the negative. A parish I once served has had a parochial school for over sixty years. If the school were to close tomorrow, there would be an old person somewhere who was against having a school from its inception, who would say, "I told them that it wouldn't work."

But these kinds of people are hopeless, right? "No!" God says. Love hopes all things and does not give up on anyone or anything. God's love, through us, seeks out even the negative people. It does not cease in its constant effort to bring out the best in them.

Our world is filled with difficult situations and difficult people. They provide us with abundant opportunities to practice the Christian virtue of love and forgiveness as well as opportunities to exercise hope in all things.

God expects the best from everyone. Behind even the worst exterior, God can see a child that was not loved enough; one whose development was stunted because someone ceased believing in her. When we put our faith in people, we give them the courage to mature and reach their potential. Those given up as hopeless withdraw into themselves and build a protective shell around themselves which never allows them to taste the full sweetness of life.

Even in the hardest heart, in the crustiest creature, in the worst person, is the soul of a child of God. Kindness inspired by the love of God hangs in even with these people until the spark of our love once again rekindles the good in them. Love may not be able to give a good reason for its hopefulness, but it nevertheless does not give up hoping.

"What shall we do with this worthless bum?" asked the doctor in Latin during the Middle Ages. Before him lay a victim of poverty who had been picked up for dead and sent to the clinic for medical experimentation.

To everyone's surprise, the supposedly dead man suddenly regained consciousness just as the above question was being asked. In Latin he answered them, "Do not call worthless someone for whom Christ died." He had been a learned man who had fallen on difficult times. Nevertheless, he still was a priceless child of God for whom Christ had given his life.

Christ died for all, hoping that all would receive him as their Lord and Savior. Christ does not love some more than others but loves all equally and wishes the very best for everyone. The virtue of love must love that which is deemed unlovable, forgive that which is thought unforgivable, and hope for that which seems hopeless, or there is no virtue at all. Love never gives up; it never accepts defeat; it searches until it finds some reason to continue hoping. This positive attitude is embodied in a Japanese haiku that reads,

My barn having burned down,
I can now see the moon

Karl Menninger, the renowned American psychiatrist, noted that if no one believes the patient can get well, there probably won't be any recovery. To live without hope is to cease to live. Several thousand years before Menninger, Pliny, an early Roman author, wrote that hope is the pillar that holds up the world.

Julia Ward Howe Embodied Hope

On November 18, 1861, early in the Civil War, the Lord began to speak a beautiful word of hope to a fractured American society as a woman by the name of Julia Ward Howe slept fitfully while troops marched in the streets below. As she lay awake waiting for the dawn, the words of a beautiful poem began to fashion themselves in her thoughts. The memory of some of the greatest lines in the Old Testament came to her mind and mingled with the faces of soldiers sitting around campfires and battle trumpets recently sounded.

The cost of the Civil War had not been counted; the horror of the war had not been foreseen. It had been entered upon almost with a giddy fervor. And the initial excitement had given way to determination and the solemn acceptance of sacrifice.

She got out of bed and began to write, "Mine eyes have seen the glory of the coming of the Lord"… and minutes later a beautiful gospel message flowed from her pen,

In the beauty of the lilies, Christ was born across the sea, With a glory in his bosom that transfigures you and me: As he died to make men holy, let us live to make men free, While God is marching on.

It was over a year before her poem was discovered and set to a familiar tune that the soldiers knew. Very quickly it was being sung in many army regiments. On one occasion a Chaplain McCabe sang it at a mass meeting in Washington. The audience joined in on the chorus,

Glory! Glory! Hallelujah!
Glory! Glory! Hallelujah!
Glory! Glory! Hallelujah!
While God is marching on.

The effect was magical as people wept and sang together. Above the applause was heard the voice of Abraham Lincoln. Tears unashamedly rolled down his cheeks as he shouted, "Sing it again!"

Julia Ward Howe was a beautiful Christian lady who permitted God to use her to present the gospel of hope to her troubled world. Even during the bleakest moments of history, Christians have the wonderful hope that extends even beyond the grave into the glory of God's heavenly tomorrow.

There is not a hopeless situation or person. As one of my favorite hymns proclaims,

> *My hope is built on nothing less*
> *than Jesus' blood and righteousness...*
> *On Christ, the solid rock, I stand,*
> *all other ground is sinking sand..*

With our feet firmly planted upon the solid rock of Jesus Christ, our love hopes all things.

Reflection

1) Why is the word "hopeless" such a sad word?

2) Tell of something in your own life that you felt hopeless about and with God's help, it turned around.

3) Someone has said, "There are few hopeless situations; there are only hopeless attitudes." Why is this mostly true?

4) It is said that perhaps a third of all Christian churches will hopelessly close in the next ten years. What might Christians do better to keep this from happening?

5) Give an example or two from the life of Christ when he turned around a hopeless situation.

6) Why is there no such thing as a worthless person?

7) Is there someone in your church that is so difficult that people have referred to them as hopeless? With God's help, how might you help this person?

8) Why is it true that to cease to live without hope, is to cease to live?

9) What is something significant that you are hoping for right now?

10) What is the ultimate hope that God's love has made possible for everyone?

TWELVE

Love Endures All Things

It was December 23, one of the busiest days in a pastor's life as he not only has his personal Christmas preparation to accomplish but that of the church he serves as well. On that day, Tim wandered into the church I was serving in Hicksville, New York. He wanted to talk to a pastor. He was not a member of the church, and I had never seen him before. He was an eighteen-year-old teenager.

As I invited him to come into my office, I could see that he was deeply troubled about something. His arms hung lifeless at his sides. His eyes were downcast. There was no expression in his face of the joy of Christmas just two days away.

But that was just it: Christmas was Tim's problem. He was troubled because of Christmas. "Pastor, my parents divorced when I was eleven," he began his story. "Both of them remarried, and I did not seem to fit in with either family. I lived with one of them then the other. Always there were fights. The other day I had a big fight with my father, and he threw me out of the house. Right now, I live in a small rented room." He lived in an illegitimate boarding house in town used by the down-and-out of the community. It was not a place for a young man.

As he talked, I was impressed by Tim's sincerity. His words did not flow like those from the sharp minds of the numerous con artists whose sad tales were directed at filching money from our church's treasury. His story was not leading up to the usual question, "If you could loan me just $20, I could take the bus upstate and stay with my aunt who wants me to spend Christmas with her." Rather, his sad words came from deep within an empty heart devoid of joy in a season busy proclaiming, "Joy to the world, the Lord is come."

"I can handle being thrown out of my father's house and having to live in a lousy room, except it is Christmas," Tim told me. "But the thought of families being together sharing their love and happiness and me not being a part of one is almost too much to bear." By now, his voice was choked, and his eyes glistened with restrained tears. He blew his nose.

My mind raced for solutions. Tim asked for no money; he had lodging and needed no bus fare. What he desperately needed was a family to share their love and warmth with him at Christmas. Since it was the day before Christmas Eve, this would be no small task to arrange. Coming in off the street with no connection to our parish made the job even more impossible. Christmas is a *family* time, with traditions jealously guarded.

On Christmas Eve, our family had plans to have dinner at a local restaurant with good friends. On Christmas Day, we were invited to relatives to spend the day. Our situation was like most families. Strangers and change are not readily accepted as carefully orchestrated Christmas plans were all in place. Had he been one of the many who came to our church wanting money, it would have been so easy – but he needed so much more.

"Tim, give me a little time; I think I can help," I said to him, exhibiting more confidence in my voice than was in my mind. "Come back to my office tomorrow morning at 10:00 a.m.," I urged him.

That evening, when I told my family about Tim's plight, I was proud of their willingness to include him in our Christmas Eve plans. I then called a wonderful family of our parish who had children around Tim's age. They said that they would be willing to include Tim in their Christmas Day celebration. God's hand of love was clearly at work for one of his hurting children.

When Tim returned to my office on Christmas Eve morning, I told him, "Tim, my family would love for you to join us for dinner at 1:00 p.m. this afternoon at a restaurant in town and then come to our home afterward. We have four services on Christmas Eve beginning at 6:00 p.m., so I will have to bring you back to church with me for the first service. Another family in our parish has invited you to join them Christmas Day after the morning worship service." Although Tim offered some weak comments about not wanting to impose, the pain of staying at home alone on Christmas was so great that he quickly accepted both invitations with a smile.

Dressed very nicely, Tim came to dinner with us. My two younger daughters immediately liked him. Earlier in the day, we did some hurried shopping and had a present for Tim under our tree for when we all returned from dinner. What surprised us was that he had purchased a box of chocolates, wrapped it himself, and gave it to us when we exchanged gifts. It was becoming apparent that not only were we God's blessing for Tim but that God was blessing us through him as well.

Taking him back to church, Tim asked me if he could usher at our first Christmas Eve service. "Sure, Tim, we could really use you; church is so crowded on Christmas Eve," I enthusiastically told him. Tim ushered at our 6:00 p.m. service, greeting everyone with a warm smile and a Merry Christmas. He also stayed and ushered for the 7:30 p.m. service and the 9:00 p.m. service and even the 11:00 p.m. service – setting an all-time consecutive ushering record for our parish.

At all four services Tim joyfully shared the warmth and beauty of his love with hundreds of people. I could hardly believe this was the downcast youth who had fought back tears in my office barely 24 hours earlier.

On Christmas Day, Tim and the family who so unselfishly included him in their Christmas had a wonderful time together. They even thanked me for sending Tim their way. They, too, went out of their way and purchased a present for him – and you guessed it, Tim bought a present for them.

"Love endures all things," (1 Corinthians 13:7) Saint Paul tells us. God's love endured a creation fallen away. God's love endured a stable full of animals and a manger for a bed. Love endured a cross producing excruciating pain. Love also endured the small intrusion of a stranger named Tim into the realm of a Christmas filled with sacred moments and traditions. And because Christian love endures and gives and includes, it also receives more abundantly in return. Several of us helped make it a good Christmas for Tim. He helped make it a great Christmas for us.

Enduring Love Is Tough

Enduring love is also tough. It is like an army that is threatened with overwhelming defeat by superior numbers of the enemy, yet which steadfastly refuses to give ground. Enduring love is like seasoned timber which stands every test. It is a love that encounters stumbling blocks and turns them into stepping stones. For love to endure, it must endure. That is, for love to last, it must be willing to suffer misfortune without giving up. Despite the darkest night, it keeps looking toward the dawn.

One of the problems with love today is that it has lost the quality of longevity. If people are going to continue with each other in a relationship of love, at some point in that life-long relationship suffering and endurance is called into play. We must not be so quick to separate ourselves from each other by walking out when things get difficult.

Wives are called upon by God to love their husbands with enduring love as their husbands tell the same stories for the umpteenth time. Husbands need enduring love for their wives as they find fault with what husbands may see as non-consequential stuff. I once asked my wife, "Do I bring as much criticism to your life as you bring to mine?" To which she replied, "No, but you need it more." And I still love her.

As a kid, I can remember my mother fussing with my father for putting his cigarette ashes in every ashtray in our house. "Why don't you use just one of the ashtrays so that I do not have to clean and empty all of the rest?" Mom would constantly complain. Finally, after years of hearing this constant lament, one day I went up to my father and pleaded, "Dad, I'm really tired of hearing Mom constantly complain about the dirty ashtrays, and I bet you are too. Wouldn't it be easier for all of us if you simply put all of your ashes into one ashtray?" "Son," my wiser father answered, "if your mother weren't complaining about this, she would be complaining about something else about me. This I can handle."

Love needs to endure all things... even husbands and wives. One of the most repeated phrases in the Bible is, "for his steadfast love endures forever" (Psalm 136:1-26). In this psalm, it is repeated in all 26 verses. *Love is steadfast; it does not give up.* God calls us to hang in there... no *ifs*, *ands*, or *buts* about it.

There is a legend of an eagle swooping down and carrying off a screaming baby. It then soars to its lofty nest at the top of a cliff. One after another of the strongest men in the village tried to climb the high, treacherous cliff. One after the other failed.

Quietly, and before anyone took notice, a frail, young woman walked past these defeated men as they talked to one another wondering how they would break the sad news of their failure to the distraught family. Finally, someone noticed that the woman was struggling up the sheer precipice.

Miraculously, she reached the nest, fought off the eagle, and returned safely with the baby in her arms. "How did you do it?" the strong men asked incredulously. She told them the secret of her success: "I am the baby's mother." Her love enabled her to endure the fear of falling and even death. Love endured all things necessary to save the baby.

An American journalist in China watched a Roman Catholic nun cleansing the gangrenous sores of wounded soldiers in a hospital. "I wouldn't do that for a million dollars," the journalist said. Without pausing in her work, the sister quietly replied, "Neither would I."

Only the love of God in Jesus dwelling within us can inspire love like this. Albert Schweitzer said repeatedly that as long as there was a man in the world who was hungry, sick, lonely, or living in fear, he was his responsibility. He affirmed this belief by living a life which demonstrated his conviction. He lived a life of the highest fulfillment and one full of enduring love for his fellow humans.

Saint Paul calls upon our love to be strong and tenacious. We are not to grow weary of well doing. Loving someone difficult is hard, but love that is the greatest finds renewed strength in God. It, therefore, has the wonderful quality of endurance. As love endures, it also remembers that with God's help, victory is not far off.

Reflection

1) Why do you think Tim stayed for all four Christmas Eve services?

2) If your pastor called you to host a stranger on Christmas Day, do you think you would say "yes" or beg off?

3) Share a special Christmas memory when you were both a blessing and blessed.

4) Do you feel the less fortunate people of your community are in any way your responsibility?

5) Share how you loved someone who was difficult to love.

6) Share how someone loved you when you were difficult to love.

7) What has been difficult in your life that you have had to endure?

8) When in your life have you turned stumbling blocks into stepping stones?

9) Share a family story of enduring love.

10) How has God's steadfast love that lasts forever been a blessing to you?

THIRTEEN

Love Never Ends

Turning to the last beautiful facet of Saint Paul's love poem, it gives us joy to read, "Love never ends" (1 Corinthians 13:8). Others have translated his words, "Love never fails or disappears." How wonderful that love is eternal; it is forever, for it is the very essence of God. If love were to end, God would also have to end, for God is love. How beautifully impossible for either God or love to end. This is a wonderful reality.

The prophet Jeremiah received an appearance from the Lord, and the Lord said to him, "I have loved you with an everlasting love" (Jeremiah 31:3). God's love is everlasting and cannot end. At his ascension, Jesus promised that he would be with us always even to the close of the age. God's promise of love has always been an eternal promise. Nothing can separate the faithful from the love of God in Christ Jesus. Jesus' love is stronger than even death itself, for he loves us beyond the grave into eternity.

Love Is The Source Of Life Itself

Without love, life would not be worthwhile. Even more, without love, life would struggle to exist. There have been studies done on orphaned children who lived in institutions where all of their physical needs were met, but there was little or no human affection given to them. Without love, the mortality rate was extremely high.

One of several long-term studies was done on a dozen orphaned children. The children were split into two groups of six. Each child in the first group was brought daily to a nearby institution to be cared for and loved by an adolescent, retarded girl. The second group did not receive this kind of affection. After twenty years, a number of orphans in the second group died. Some of those who lived were in institutions for the mentally retarded or mentally ill.

The children in the first group who received love fared much better. They became self-supporting; all were married, and most had graduated high school. Love is essential for life itself.

God's love is equal to whatever negatives a sinful world throws its way. The wonder of never ending love was just praised by Saint Paul when he reminded us that love "bears all things, believes all things, hopes all things, endures all things" (1 Corinthians 13:7).

No tragedy, no trials, and no negative circumstances can destroy love. Love continues to be optimistic even when there are no grounds for optimism. There is nothing quite like love for its greatness, for it is of God. Saint John writes, "Beloved, let us love one another, because love is from God; everyone who loves is born of God and knows God" (1 John 4:7).

Love Never Quits

Dietrich Bonhoeffer, a Christian martyr during the Second World War said poignantly, "When Christ calls a man, he bids him come and die." During World War II, a soldier asked permission of his senior officer to go out into "no man's land" to retrieve one of his buddies who lay grievously wounded. The officer replied, "You can go out, but it won't be worth it. Your friend might already be dead, and you will probably lose your life as well to enemy gunfire."

The young soldier was not to be deterred. Somehow, he managed to reach his friend, hoist him on his shoulders and bring him back to the trench. In the process, a bullet found its mark in the rescuer. As they both tumbled into the trench, the brave soldier's officer said, "I told you it wouldn't be worth it, for your friend is dead and now you are badly wounded." "It was worth it, sir," the young soldier replied, "because when I got to my buddy, he was still alive, and he said, 'I knew you would come.'" Real love, like the love of Jesus Christ, continually seeks us out and never lets us down. Love never quits.

When the Bible says that God loves us, it doesn't mean that God gets romantic heart palpitations. When God considered his wayward world standing up to its nostrils in sinful muck, God didn't send a bouquet of flowers for us to smell for the last few seconds before our doom. Instead, God extended patience and unleashed infinite kindness by sending his son to become the target of spit and unmerciful ridicule – capped off by a horrendous death on Calvary.

When Jesus came to earth, it was not to bring a religion, but it was to bring his sacrificial self and his forgiving love. This is what love is at its most concentrated and potent form. The Bible puts it this way, "No one has greater love than this, to lay down one's life for one's friends" (John 15:13).

Jesus not only wants to be in our lives but desires to be the master of our lives. He wants to be in the driver's seat. If our lives were to be likened to our automobiles, where would Jesus' place be in them? Would he be in the trunk like the spare tire, to only be called forth in an emergency? Would he be in the back seat, only to be consulted occasionally for advice? Does he sit beside us, one with whom we have regular conversation? Or is he in the driver's seat, at the controls, guiding our lives as he wants them to go?

Be A Love Generator

In our world today we have been successful in harnessing the energy of fossil fuel, the sun, the wind, and even the atom for the betterment of humankind. This is great, but we must seek to better harness the greatest energy of all for the good of God's people… that is the energy of love. Each of us needs to be a love generator. We get our energy to love when we regularly attend worship and study the Lord's word. Then we are better able to offer ourselves and our love to others.

If everyone suddenly discovered that they had only five minutes left in their lives to say all they wanted to say, every telephone would be in use with people trying to phone other people to tell them they loved them.

Now is the best time to reach out and touch someone with our love — to interact with the people that God wants to love through us.

Saint Paul Concludes His Love Poem

Although Saint Paul's poem of love might have concluded with the simple and encouraging words "love never ends," he once again contrasts love with prophecy, tongues, and knowledge. These three have no permanence. Again he proclaims that love's greatness surpasses even these praised precepts. As King Solomon said in his Song of Songs, "Many waters cannot quench love; neither can rivers drown it" (Song of Solomon 8:7).

Putting away childish concepts of love and life, we grow up understanding in greater measure love's wonderful richness. This comes with Christian maturity. But with this wonderful maturity, we also realize that we have just begun to draw from the vast reservoir of God's love.

What we can now see and understand of God is only a dim image of all that God is. God's fullness can only be completely enjoyed in eternity. A full knowledge of God and a full participation in all that is God must wait until we arrive in heaven.

A poor widow contributed what seemed to be a large sum of money to her church. She was asked if that generous sum was too much for a person in her circumstances. She answered, "Love is not afraid of giving too much."

Christ demonstrated a love that gave all. Even though evil nailed incarnate love to a tree, on the third day love proved victorious over the evil that sought to destroy it. When we put selfishness behind and walk with the Lord, we participate more freely in his unfailing love. Our life in Christ becomes a life of love, and love's many facets are not only ours to enjoy but are also ours on which to reflect. Like a beautiful diamond, we too can sparkle. A life full of love is the best possible life of all.

Love — It's The Greatest!

"And now, faith, hope and love abide, these three; and the greatest of these is love" (1 Corinthians 13:13). Lifting up the three great virtues of faith, hope, and love brings Saint Paul's love poem to a fitting close. Faith in God is the source of our hope for eternal life. Both of these are eternally important and are in no way diminished by Paul in his last verse. Nevertheless, Saint Paul once again proclaims love's supremacy over all other virtues, for love will continue even into eternity. In time, faith will be replaced by knowledge, and our hope will be fulfilled when Christ returns, but love will always remain... because love is the greatest virtue of them all. It will never end.

Reflection

1) How does it make you feel that nothing can separate you from the love of God?

2) Why does love continue to be optimistic even when there are no grounds for optimism?

3) What do you think Bonhoeffer meant when he said that when Christ calls us to be his disciples, he bids us to come and die?

4) How does God love you with his never-ending love?

5) Is God in the driver's seat of your life?

6) How might your life generate more love?

7) How has your love matured over the years?

8) Why is love greater than either faith or hope?

9) How does selfishness get in the way of love?

10) Having read this book, what might God be calling you to do right now?

About The Author

John Krahn has been a pastor for nearly fifty years. He was the pastor of the largest multi-staffed Lutheran church in New York for eighteen years. During his long ministry, he was the CEO of The United Lutheran Appeal, the Director of Admissions at L.I. Lutheran High School, an Army Chaplain, the owner of his own business, and the interim pastor for many struggling churches.

He is currently a parish consultant specializing in stewardship and evangelism. He is also a much published writer.

Krahn has a Doctorate in Ministry degree from New York Theological Seminary, New York; a Masters of Divinity degree from Concordia Seminary in Saint Louis; a Masters of Educational and Theological Studies degree from Union Theological Seminary, New York; and a Master of Education degree from Columbia University, New York.

www.ingramcontent.com/pod-product-compliance
Lightning Source LLC
Chambersburg PA
CBHW022027090426
42739CB00006BA/313

*9 7 8 0 7 8 8 0 2 9 3 0 1 *